AF280075

Personal biography
Stefan Asemota
with photos by the Author

Publisher: BoD · Books on Demand GmbH,
In de Tarpen 42, 22848 Norderstedt, bod@bod.de
Print: Libri Plureos GmbH, Friedensallee 273,
22763 Hamburg
ISBN: 978-3-7583-6980-3

CHINESE OF AFRICA

Bibliographic information from the German National Library: The German National Library lists this publication in the German National Bibliography; detailed bibliographic data is available on the Internet at http://dnb.dnb.de.

Publisher: BoD · Books on Demand GmbH, In de Tarpen 42, 22848 Norderstedt, bod@bod.de

Print: Libri Plureos GmbH, Friedensallee 273, 22763 Hamburg
ISBN: 978-3-7583-6980-3

D E D I C A T I O N

---

for Osaze, Ebun
for my parents
my grandfather Epa Adun, whom I never knew
and Nigeria in mortification

E P I G R A P H

Agha biẹ ọmọ, ọmọ ghi vbe biẹ ọmwan
When you birth a child, he or she later births you.

— *Edo parable*

P R E F A C E

I wasn't prepared to lose my mother on the 1st of March 2021, but it was one of those many things in life that comes at you unexpectedly.

My mother, Klara Asemota, was the pillar of our multifaceted cultural family—a caring, compassionate Swiss woman who stood by my father even when others didn't understand their union. Though it wasn't always easy growing up from a mixed background, Mother shielded us from the harshest prejudices through her fierce love. I revered her kindness and deeply cherished our closeness, in contrast to the emotional distance I felt from my father.

So when dementia took her life far too soon, at age 75, the hole left in my heart was gaping. I grieved the finality of never hearing her lilting voice again or seeking her nurturing advice. In my sorrow, I turned to my father, hoping our shared loss might bridge the divide of unfamiliarity that had separated us for most of my life. That pivotal decision led me on a journey with him to Nigeria, a complex nation with over 200 million diverse people and cultures.

Nicknamed "the giant of Africa" for its massive population on the continent, Nigeria is just like China. Not in terms of development or growth, but in the potential it holds. With over 200 million people, Nigeria is the world's most populous "Black Country." Similarly, China's 1.4 billion population makes it one of the world's most populous nations as well. Both countries have faced challenges in converting their large populations into economic engines.

While one has succeeded, the other has failed, and, in fact, Nigeria continues to struggle with poverty, inequality, and poor governance. China has leveraged its massive workforce to become an economic powerhouse and a global manufacturer. In contrast, despite an abundance of natural resources that should make Nigeria the wealthiest country on the continent, systemic government corruption and infrastructural decay have stunted socioeconomic gains for most citizens.

In these pages, I chronicle not only my experience of losing my mother and my travel back to Nigeria, but also my deep thoughts, opinions, hallucinations, memories, and countless battles of confronting social injustices as a bicultural person of Nigerian and Swiss origin.

This book is about the scars, illuminated truths, and cemented facts about my personal odyssey of grief, connection, and revelation in Nigeria. It covers the emotional wounds that may never fully heal after losing my mother, but also the perspectives I gained on life's unpredictable nature. It will show some of the harsh realities of my father's homeland that were obscured from an outsider's view—poverty, corruption, infrastructure collapse—and my shift from naivety to nuanced understanding.
It's about quiet moments on the streets of Cuba that revealed generosity of spirit amid hardship, challenging preconceived notions. And confronting my complex relationship with being bicultural, neither fully my mother's son nor my father's, and realising identity comes from within.

It's about honesty—seeing my father as a fully flawed human being, not the distant figure I blamed for my isolation as a child. And finding empathy for decisions I may never agree with.
It's about understanding my mother's remarkable courage in building a life in Nigeria as a foreign white woman in the 1970s, the trials she endured, and the dreams she held. And Honoring her memory by embracing that same spirit while hoping that maybe, just maybe, Nigeria can one day become the "Chinese of Africa".

13

A C K N O W L E D G E M E N T S

I want to express my deep gratitude to Nigeria, the land that has shaped my identity. Being Nigerian is no simple story—it's a journey of raw emotions, where pride and anger live side by side, where challenges and victories are part of our daily lives. It means facing a society's broken systems, and sadly, my family foreman, Peter, knows this truth all too well.

This acknowledgement is more than just a thank you to those who inspired me to write this book. It's also a tribute to Peter's recent loss. His newborn daughter, Obere, arrived on November 11th, 2024, at 10:23 pm, just moments after her twin sister. Three days later, on November 14th, she passed away because of the inefficiency and ineffectiveness of healthcare services in Benin City.

Sadly, neonatal morbidity and mortality rates are very high in Nigeria. This also reflects the many struggles in the country, as you'll see in this book.

With that said, I would start by acknowledging my wife: Thank you for your unwavering support. Caught in between my Nigerian and Swiss roots, you've always been my backbone. Your understanding has guided me through finding myself, and for this I'm forever grateful.

To my sons, you're my greatest joy. Your laughter, lessons, and love have lit up my world, and your very existence has helped me understand life's complicated moments.

I'm grateful to Success, my editor, whose sharp eye and careful work have improved this book. Your honest feedback has been a true gift.

To Thomas of the Cosmos, thank you for creating an avenue where we can tell our true stories without holding back.

And to my brother, your way of solving problems instead of complaining has always inspired me. Your words, "Let's see how we can fix this" are how you show your love and support to those around you. I am grateful!

As I look back on this work, I see Nigeria—a story of pain and hope, of hard times and moments of joy. We are a people who don't just survive but push forward no matter what. This book is my way of telling that story, and I hope you enjoy every chapter.

O W O | 1

Death has a way of dampening any man's soul. It is our most dreaded enemy and our closest reminder of the forgotten value of having a life. As someone who lost his mother at the most unexpected time in his life, I can attest to the terrible emotional condition that comes with such a loss. It was as if everything was falling apart, and there seemed to be no way out. I tried to forget about the whole thing as if nothing had happened, and that meant living in denial about what had befallen me.

People kept asking me how I felt, but I did not feel like discussing it because the more I thought about it, the more it broke my heart; so, I preferred they observe my mood and just let me be! But that never happened. It only grew worse as they continued calling and texting to express their understanding of how I was feeling and to let me know that they, too, had lost a loved one at some point in their lives. I was mourning in grief and in a state of emotional suffering. The small talk they saw as a remedy stood little prospect of aiding me in this period of discomfort and pain.

Losing my mother at that point in time meant losing a big part of myself. It felt like something in me died with her that day. I felt a sudden transition inside of me. A feeling of darkness had now filled a space where love once was.

I wish I had quit and just cried. I wish I had lessened my masculinity for a moment and expressed how battered I was. Maybe I would have done it indoors where no one would watch, but I knew the implications this would bring. I knew it would only get worse and force me to break the promise I made to her years before she passed away—a promise to stay strong for my children—her grandchildren, irrespective of the circumstances.

Osaigbovo! Osaigbovo! Osaigbovo!!

I felt a push on my shoulder, and a familiar voice calling my native name. It was my father.

Yes... Yes, Father?!

You've been staring at the hostess since. She is asking if you would like a cup of coffee.

Oh! Sorry! I would appreciate that. Thank you. I said with a clouded smile to hide the worry on my face

She tapped me on the shoulder with a smile, too, so I assumed she may have guessed that I was going through a lot.

Okay! I will be right back, she said, and strolled away.

Is everything okay, son? My father asked with an anxious look.

I was so engrossed in my thoughts that I became unaware of my surroundings, but that was no reason to remind my father of our loss.

Yes, I'm fine. I said as I relaxed back to take a nap.

We were on a flight headed to Nigeria. My father was returning from Switzerland, where he had been by my beloved mother's side during her last moments on earth. This trip felt like his last international journey, and I felt a need to accompany him. It was important to be there for him during this time.

After my mother's death, he decided it was time he returned to his beloved country. He wanted this journey to be a reunion between us, so he told me to accompany him back to Nigeria.

In fact, let me rewind to a couple of months prior to this trip, when I made the decision to follow him. We were together, having a stroll somewhere in the city of Bern. That day, we made a stop at a cafe just ahead of us to grab something to drink. As we sat down, my father started reminiscing heartfelt stories about when he first met my mother.

Initially, the conversation was going well, and I was eager to hear all he had to say. We barely had moments like these, so I was ready to enjoy every bit, but my father was so engrossed in his memories, which he poured into each verse of this grand story, that he forgot, or I assumed he forgot, that he was talking to his son and not one of his childhood buddies.

His reminiscing took on a creepier tone when he started describing my mother's physique. That was when I knew it was time to draw the line on this one.

Her lips were so beautiful that you could never stop gazing at...

Hmmm, Father? I interrupted him.

Yes?

*What do you think is wrong with the political system in Nigeria? I responded
by trying to change the topic.*

Political system in Nigeria?

Yes, Father, the Nigerian political system, I reiterated.

*I'm talking about the love of my life, and you are asking me
about the political system in Nigeria?*

He seemed very furious, like a man woken up from an enjoyable sleep, but I was resolute about changing the topic because it felt weirder every minute he unfolded his youthful flings with my mother. I mean, I would have hoped he censored some parts of that story, but he just kept on filling me with unfiltered and definitely uncensored experiences he had with her.

Yeah, Father, she is my mother too, you know?

*Oh!, hahahahahahahaha, he laughed hard. It seemed he had now
understood the reason for my deviation.*

One thing I love about my father is his ability to detect intent during any conversation. He can tell what you want to say even without you saying it, and that has made him a good conversationalist over the years.
We changed the topic and began discussing the political systems in Nigeria. My father had only three hobbies he loved, which were reading, jogging, and discussing politics with his friends and sometimes with me. He groomed my political knowledge and interests right from when I was a child. I used to observe him discussing with his friends either on a call or when they came around the house, so gradually his philosophies became my philosophies, although mine are more refined with modern-day innovations. As we were discussing, he paused and looked at me.

Would you mind accompanying me back to Nigeria?

he asked, his voice filled with a mix of sadness and hope.

*Your mother is no longer with us, and I believe she would want us to reunite our bonds
as father and son.*

He took a moment to observe my reaction before continuing,

*I know you are a grown man with so much to do, but I appeal to you to honour my
request.*

He knew with that well-laid speech he just gave there was no way I was going to deny him, and besides that, my father and I had not really hung out much since I was a child, so I expected this journey would definitely be full of emotions as it might be the last international trip my father would make. So I thought to myself,

Why not grant the old man his last international travel request?

Fast-forward to now. It is the Corona virus breakout era (COVID-19). The weather at our destination was 35 degrees Celsius. My father and I had been sitting comfortably for the last 6 hours and were about to land in Lagos, Nigeria.

We were happy to arrive at the Murtala Muhammed International Airport (MMIA) for two reasons. One, my father did not enjoy travelling, and two, we had encountered a couple of obstacles while planning this trip.

Because of COVID-19 travel regulations for Nigeria, authorised inbound foreign passengers were required to submit a negative result from a COVID-19 polymerase chain reaction (PCR) test (costing around 156 Swiss Francs) taken only 72 hours before boarding at the first port of departure. All inbound passengers were also required to register online at the Nigeria International Travel Portal, following all instructions and meeting all requirements, which included completing a health questionnaire, providing in-country contact information, uploading COVID-19 test results, and paying processing fees of 70 Swiss Francs.
Unfortunately, our initial flight from Basel was on a Saturday morning, so I attempted to register on Friday but was unsuccessful. I tried restlessly all night, but there was still no improvement. The website was down, and I could not get our trip's Quick Response (QR) codes.

It was a very stressful scenario that lasted until the morning of our scheduled departure. It seemed as if fate had special intentions for us. I tried all I could to register, but the website was slow or not responding at all. The check-in for our flight had now opened, and we had to present ourselves at the check-in desk to protest to the Air France officials on duty about our inability to get our QR codes.

After hearing what we had to say, the officials tried to create a sample register, but the result was the same as ours. It was a startling experience for us, but luckily, we were able to rebook the flights and get our QR codes.
Landing at the Murtala Muhammed International Airport was smooth, and the taxi ride to our gate was quick. Seatbelt signs were turned off, and passengers started embarking. Since my father required wheelchair assistance, we had to wait for our wheelchair-Uber.

He arrived shortly after, welcomed us, and encouraged my father to take a seat. He guided us through the tunnels, the COVID-19 health and QR code inspections, and the passport checks. We made our way to the baggage claim and awaited our bags. Because we had three bags, I figured it would be a good plan to get a trolley.

In Nigeria, you need cash for everything! The major problem is getting a hold of this "cash." So, I told my father that I was going to get some money because I did not have enough with me and we needed it for the hotel. After asking him to take a seat and wait, I began searching for the nearest Automated Teller Machine (ATM) terminal I could lay my hands on. Fortunately, I was able to find one.

As I approached the ATM, only one of them had a very long queue; the other had the "unable to dispense cash" message on the screen. After a tireless wait of twenty minutes, it was my turn, and I inserted my First Bank of Nigeria card only to be greeted with a message: "Your card is inactive or not accepted." It had been years since I last used the card, so I assumed it may have been deactivated and inserted another card (from a different bank). This time, it requested my pin, so I felt everything was fine, perhaps even too perfect, until I selected the withdrawal amount of just 60,000 Naira (₦) and pushed the "OK" button.

As the teller machine was processing my request, I began imagining how valuable ₦60,000 would have been if it shared the same value with other foreign currencies, like the dollar and euro. Imagine how wealthy I would have been right now. The beep on the ATM brought an end to my short-lived thoughts. Unfortunately, this particular ATM had now developed a cash dispensing issue. I was damned! Welcome to the homeland. I returned to find my father patiently awaiting me, amusing himself with the to-and-fro movement at the spot where he sat.
"Why did it take so long?" he asked as he saw me approaching. I told him about the situation at the ATM, and the next thing I heard was him yelling angrily, "Still? This sort of nonsense is still happening in this country."

This would have been a glorious moment to debate him because, just a few hours ago, he was bragging about how good the systems work in Nigeria and how Buhari is changing everything. He could now see for himself how hard things were in the country he claimed was working fine, and I did not feel the urge to poke him any further. Instead, I grabbed the little cash from my wallet and made my way to the trolley dispatcher.

Arriving there, I noticed everyone was paying something to get it, so I asked how much it would cost. He said, "₦1500." Luckily for me, our wheelchair-Uber guy gave me a hint, which was ₦150. I then replied sarcastically, "Only ₦1500?" The trolley dispatcher guy quickly understood that I was not some foreigner to be scammed. He stood there staring at me, trying not to react facially or say anything that could escalate things.

Seeing the fear on his face, I told him, "I will be back in a second," and left, suddenly deciding I could do without one. My father and I walked to the baggage claim section and waited over an hour to collect our bags before making our way to the customs for our final clearance.
As we approached the customs, one of their officers flagged us down. "Please come this way," he said. It was obvious they had no plans to examine our documents or anything

else but were seeking to extort us. The next thing this officer said to us was, "Wetin you bring for me?"

I was in no mood to entertain such friendliness or questions, so I said, "You send me message?" The officer smiled and eventually let us go without even inspecting any of our luggage. We were glad and headed for the exit. The last point of inspection was the verification of our luggage tags and our boarding tickets to ensure that we were not taking someone else's luggage.

After going through all that stress, we made our way to the exit and got swamped by taxi drivers who were hunting for customers. Travellers who had no one to pick them up at the airport were at the mercy of these drivers, who would do anything to make you hire their cabs. Their voices were the first thing you would hear as soon as you exit the arrival lounge. The disorderly manner in which they swamped travellers is just a snippet of how disorganised the country is and what you can expect as soon as you leave the airport.

Luckily for us, Teddy, a childhood friend of mine, had planned for a taxi to come pick us up, so we did not have to consider any of the crazy drivers at the airport. While I was about to send him a text to let him know we had arrived, my phone alerted me about a ₦60,000 transaction. I did not understand the context of the text message because the ATM I tried earlier did not dispense any cash.

I checked the message source to see if it was from my bank, and it was, so I ignored it and called Teddy instead. He told me the driver was on his way and his name was Ayo. In less than five minutes after the call, Ayo drove to us and helped with the bags as well as ensured my father was comfortably seated. He seemed like a shy guy initially, but we later discovered that he had a jovial personality.

The ride to the hotel was approximately forty minutes, but we could not even tell because Ayo filled every minute with intriguing tales from his experiences. He used to be a teacher in Edo State, where his best friend, who came from a far wealthier family, taught him how to drive. He moved to Lagos to live with his aunt, and his uncle in-law bought a car for her. Because she did not know how to drive or had any intention of learning or using the car, Ayo persuaded her to give him the keys. That is how his self-employment journey started.

As we departed, I could see the image of the airport swallowed up by the darkness of the night in the rearview mirror. Upon arriving at our hotel in Ikeja, I helped Ayo remove our bags from his car. I pressed some cash into his hands, and we parted ways. We were staying just one night at this Catholic mission, a three-star hotel that offered not only airport drop-off transfer, a restaurant, concierge, and shoe-shining service, but also a casino, an aqua park, and a golf course. It was pretty well equipped for a three-star hotel.

While I was moving our bags to the hotel's reception, I noticed a tear in my father's right eye. I could not tell at that moment if he was sad and upset about my mother's absence or if he needed his eye medication. I wiped his tears and started a conversation with him as we walked to the reception. He later told me he always stayed at this hotel with her whenever they travelled to Lagos.

While I handled the paperwork, he was engaged in a small talk with the receptionists. He kept wiggling his legs and telling them jokes, and they were laughing together. I was glad he found something to cheer himself up, but I still do not know why he wiggles his legs so much. Sometimes it seems to be an obvious, perpetual habit, while other times it is a subtle, situational tremor. Regardless, several completely natural reasons may explain his behaviour, and I feel it is just his way of managing anxiety or excitement.

E V A | 2

I woke to my father's loud shouting.

Osaigbovo... Osaigbovo, where are you? he called out to me.

Lagiesan, I am in my room sleeping! I yelled out so he could hear me.

We were back in our home in Benin from Lagos, and as usual, my father, in his feel-at-home routine, was always the first to wake up.

Tell Bola to prepare breakfast immediately; I am starving, he yelled back, leaving me worried.

It is just short of six a.m., sir!

And so what? I'm hungry; just make it happen!

Alright! I replied while lying on my bed, contemplating what to do next.

They say the early bird gets the worm, but in this case, there was no worm to get because Bola, (our family chef) was yet to resume work and I was still feeling very sleepy. She usually started her shift at eight in the morning, but I guess my father forgot or he just wanted me to prepare his meal. Since we arrived in Nigeria, I planned on establishing the ideal morning ritual for myself, doing some yoga as soon as I wake up and jogging around our neighbourhood, but with the way things were going, that would have to be paused for now.

It took me roughly three minutes, a few noises from the living room and some mumblings to realise that I was the one he wanted to prepare his meal. I tried getting up, but midway I fell back to sleep, only to be awakened a few minutes later with another scream, "Is breakfast ready?" Using my mobile phone as a torchlight, I went downstairs to the kitchen, where I prepared two eggs, two slices of bread, boiled hot water for tea, opened a can of milk and finally cooked some akamu served with two cubes of sugar. Akamu, or Pap, is one of the common meals in any Nigerian household. This starchy food, made entirely of carbohydrates, originates from corn.

I arranged everything on a tray and took it upstairs to the family sitting room. To my surprise, he had already taken his seat, waiting impatiently, legs wiggling. Placed the tray on the table before him and discharged myself to the next available seat.

> *Ah, finally, thank you, He said excitedly as I pulled out a chair to sit.*
> *Have you called your bank to verify the transaction alert*
> *you received at the airport?*

> *No, not yet, I replied, while scrolling through my phone.*

> *And why is that? he inquired, this time focusing all his attention on me and*
> *ignoring the food She was eating.*

> *I have been busy with other things. We do not have a driver,*
> *no security or cleaning staff, and our solar power system*
> *is not charging properly, to name a few, I explained to him.*

> *Oh, yes, that is true. He said and continued his meal.*

> *I also noticed something yesterday. The mahogany wooden floor*
> *in this dining room is affected by termites! I think we need*
> *to replace it.*

He stopped eating and looked around as if he had just remembered something.

> *Fine. Organise it with our foreman, Peter.*

> *Alright, sir.*

There was silence in the room for some minutes as he picked his meal and occasionally stared at me. I could tell even while I was engaged in the activity on my phone.

> *Did you notice how stressful our check-in experience at the airport was the*
> *day before yesterday? my father asked, seeking to spark a conversation.*

> *Hmmm, I replied, nodding slowly in agreement.*

> *I still don't understand why the check-in process was*
> *that long. In Europe, you arrive at the check-in counter and*
> *present your passport, luggage, or bags. In no time, you are*
> *handed your boarding passes, and you leave. But here,*
> *it's another case. May God help this country.*

Amen, I said sarcastically as I watched him complain to me as if he was not one of the biggest supporters of the current government.
He gave me a slightly stern look and warned,

It is too early to be looking for my trouble.

You know, with issues like these, I will always look for your trouble, Father. After all, you strongly support President Buhari and his outdated ideas.

You have started again, this guy. Okay, Osaigbovo, can you tell me what Buhari has to do with a failed airport operating system? Is he the head of operations at the Murtala Mohammed airport? How does he even relate to what we are discussing this morning? he asked, paying full attention to me for the second time as if he were awaiting a public lecture.

Well, it's a good thing you asked. Just so you know, Nigeria's bureaucratic problems are embedded in her political history, and your dearest friend Buhari has played an active role in all of it. Let me explain it this way to you, I said as I dropped my phone on the table and pulled my chair closer.

Although Nigeria adopted the American presidential system in 1979, I continued,
Bureaucracy in different sectors continues to be shrouded in fundamental historical issues unique to Nigeria. These issues are its colonial heritage, the prevalent diarchy of the civil and military bureaucracies for over five decades now since Nigeria's independence, and the intractable challenge of the Nigerian multi-ethnic nationalities competing for resources, which accounts for a large segment of the problems affecting the country. I further explained, Father, you would agree with me that almost every administrative task in Nigeria is complex, from getting your driver's licence to getting a passport or even getting your personal National Identification Number (NIN), and yet innocent public administrators are the ones to blame with so many miraculous expectations from them to produce good results out of bad working conditions and systems, and success out of unavoidable failure at any cost. I mean, come on...

I agree with some points you shared, he quickly interrupted.
...and I propose we postpone this talk until you return from your daily business. It's already half seven. You should start heading out soon, he suggested.

I tapped on my phone to see what the time was, and realised that I had spent close to an hour talking with him, so I took my leave immediately.

Glancing through the window in my room, the sky was pitch black, and enormous clouds were heading toward me. I heard a tapping on the roof, which turned into a pitter-patter. As the clouds spit forth their water droplets, people hurried for protection indoors, and those still walking had their umbrellas opened. As the rain fell harder, puddles formed. The vehicle roofs swirled with spray, and I could hear the rain whispering through the glass. It sounded like furious bees buzzing.

Despite the heavy rain, I had to go to my bank. Two of my bank cards had expired, and I was concerned that one of them might be temporarily deactivated because of little or no transaction activity.

> *Father, where is the second umbrella? I called out to him in the living room, where he was now watching the early morning news.*
>
> *Check my bedroom; it should be behind the door.*

I was looking for a spare umbrella for Peter, who would accompany me to the bank to renew my card. Peter was our foreman and a close family friend who always had my back whenever I was in town.
The two banks were just a stone's throw from my home, so I assumed we could conclude the renewals within an hour. Well, it was eight a.m. in the ancient city of Benin. Anything was bound to happen at this chilled hour of the day.

We finally got to the premises of the First Bank of Nigeria (FBN) despite the heavy downpour that tried to stop us. Because of COVID-19, a security guard took my body temperature, and I was instructed to sanitise my hands and wear my face-mask as I would in any other public place. The same applied to Peter, who was with me.

We entered the bank without filling out any forms, and we were able to navigate our way upstairs to start our demands. My card renewal issue was quickly attended to, and I was asked to present my identification.

The bank clerk picked up 2 forms from his lower drawers and started filling them out for me. He asked me for my account number and BVN, but I told him I couldn't remember it, nor could I remember the Bank Verification Number (BVN) assigned to me before I travelled out. He later found my account number with the help of the old card I gave him and presented me with the forms he was filling earlier so I could review and sign.

> *Mr Stefan, give these to the lady downstairs, he said, while handing me some documents.*
>
> *Which one? I asked curiously.*

> *The one at the customer service desk, Miss Evelyn, is her name, he pointed out.*

> *Oh! Okay, I replied as I headed out of his office.*

I was glad this was going smoothly. Hallelujah!

Upon arriving at her desk, she kindly asked me to have a seat, and she pulled out 2 other forms, which I instantly filled out. The lady then requested one passport photo, which I didn't have. She told me that there was a photographer just opposite the bank.

"Whoops, it seems this would not be as easy as I expected," I thought to myself. I quickly signalled to Peter, who was lost in the magazine he was reading, and we made our way towards the bank's exit. The new destination, which was not part of our original plans, was the Benin-Agbor road, where the photographers' studio was situated. We arrived at the studio, knocked at the open door, and entered. To my surprise, the studio was well-decorated and spaced, unlike the usual photo studios in Nigeria. It had two sections:

To my right was a stage platform with a stool. The second part was where some computers, printers, and other equipment were arranged. The energy in the room reminded me of the 80s. There was a lovely old hand-written sign board displaying the photographer's skills. An elderly man with a well-ironed shirt sat behind one of the old computers, so I guessed he owned the place.

> *Hello! the man hailed at us with a soft smile.*

> *Good day, sir, I greeted.*

> *How can I help you, young man?*

> *I am here to take some passport photographs, I informed him.*

He told me he usually produces 8 pieces and nothing less. I said "okay" to acknowledge it wouldn't be a problem.

After the photographer took my picture, he went to the back of his studio to put on the generator. Then, he started his Windows desktop to view and process my passport photos.

The process took about ten minutes, and the gentleman handed me 8 copies for 700 Naira. I thanked him for his seamless service and asked what his name was. He replied, "Miraculous." How appropriate—his service had indeed been miraculous.

We finally got back to the bank to continue the process. All went well except for my signature, which the bank clerk said was different. She said I needed to apply for a signature change.

> *How is this even possible? I retorted.*
>
> *It's our standard bank procedure, sir, she said, trying to convince me.*
>
> *But look at these signatures, for crying out loud. Don't they look the same to you? I pointed out to her.*

We had spent over an hour and thirty minutes arguing. The lady insisted I continue signing repeatedly until my signature matched the one on their system. I could not afford to waste more time arguing with her, so I tried to make it work. I glanced through the 5th application form and re-signed it until it matched. The clerk then presented me with a new form and told me to sign or re-sign my "new signature".

After we finally resolved the signature issue, she said I should wait for the manager to approve my application. I felt like I had found myself in a job interview!

After waiting for around two hours for the manager, I was asked to walk into his office for visual approval. He asked me a few questions and validated my form. Despite that much wasted time, no new card was given to me. I would still have to return to the bank (on a rescheduled date) to pick it up.

I must say, Nigeria's "Information Technology" systems are just ineffective. Filling out five forms just to request a card renewal is totally inefficient. To make matters worse, all the forms had the account number and BVN as required fields, which I found repetitive and unnecessary. There's no disputing the fact that there are a lot of irregularities, and the entire system needs to be revamped.

To withdraw cash, I had to fill out another form, line up, and submit it to the cashier. As I waited in line at the withdrawal queue, I kept imagining if this was the experience I would get at the other bank that I was planning to renew my second bank card. Will they stall my time this long? If so, can I collect my activated card today?

After withdrawing some money, I discussed it with Peter, and we decided it was better we got something to eat first before moving on to the next bank, considering we did not know how long we would be there.

The plan was to ensure that I had at least one functioning bank card by the end of the day. Since FBN had disappointed me, it was crucial that we gave my other bank a chance, especially considering its proximity to where I currently was.

Before embarking on that journey, Peter and I quickly branched into a fast-food joint nearby to have our brunch. The rain had reduced, but I still felt it drizzling on my skin. After eating, we headed to my second bank to request my card.
We were asked to walk through a man-trapped security booth. Only one person at a time can go through and come out on the other side. The security system didn't beep as I walked through, even though I had my house keys and some coins with me (apparently, the object detection was turned off or not functioning properly). I crossed and shook my head in disbelief, wondering why the bank's management had refused to address the most critical aspect of their security system.

As we entered the main hall, we made our way to the customer relations officer and asked where the card renewals were done. The officer directed us to go upstairs. We went upstairs and found a long waiting line in the form of a T-shape. I could already see the frustration on Peter's face as he exhaled slowly through his mouth.

Poor guy. He would not have gone through all this mess if the banking systems in Nigeria could simplify their so-called "procedures" for once. The horizontal line in the T represented three clerk desks, while the vertical line represented the queue. I went up to the clerk on the right and inquired about card renewals. He handed me a form to fill out and also suggested I join the queue after completing the form.

After waiting in the queue for over an hour, it finally got to my turn, and I went forward to sit and wait for someone to attend to me.

> *What's your name, sir? a young man asked as he walked towards me.*

> *Stefan! I replied.*

> *Your account number?*

> *I'm sorry, but I can't recall it by heart.*

He then asked for my identification and old bank card, which I gave him. He found my account number and started cross-checking some details on his computer.

> *Alright, sir. Proceed to the other end of the line and meet with the staff member there. She will print out your card, he said as he pointed at the far left of the rectangular desk.*

> *Okay, thank you very much, I replied, walking out of the line for the next person.*

It took an extra twenty minutes for my card to be printed and given to me. It was saddening to imagine the stress Peter and I endured just to get an ATM card. Because of the bureaucratic tendency in Nigeria, most public and private sector workers have a poor attitude towards work, which has an overbearing adverse effect on the quality of service to clients. In the same vein, bureaucratic processes and poor work ethics have bedevilled the entire public sector of our Nigerian economy. From observation, not only the Civil Service but virtually all other public parastatals, ministries, and agencies are symbolic of delayed and slow attention for quality and efficient service delivery, and the Nigeria healthcare system is not an exemption!

> *Nigeria no be small tin oh, I cheered out to Peter, who was already showing signs of exhaustion.*

> *Oga, na so our daily bread be for Nigeria, every day unnecessary hustle, he replied with a smile.*

In both banks we visited, I had to deal with over 3 bank clerks (plus a messenger clerk responsible for dropping off and picking up stuff). I see the bureaucratic processes in Nigeria as a lousy implementation of the Rapid Planning Method (RPM), which has "chunking" as one of its core time management components. Every bureaucratic process in Nigeria is chunked into "smaller" pieces of chunks. These, be it a check-in counter at a local airport or admission at a nearby hospital, are all features of dysfunctional bureaucracy in Nigeria, which always proves to be a stumbling block to innovative ideas and improvement in the country.

My hope is for the banking experience in Nigeria to transform into a coffee shop-like atmosphere, where skilled baristas can reignite emotional connections between customers and the product. How? By reducing the administrative hurdles or processes.

> *Wetin be your plan? You still wan go factory? I asked Peter.*

> *Yes oh, I wan go prepare the mahogany wood, so dat when you come tomorrow morning you fit start with the moulding. Dat na, if National Electric Power Authority (NEPA) give us light, he replied.*

> *Okay, no wahala, take this cash for your transport fare. We go see tomorrow, I said, shoving 3 pieces of 1000 Naira notes into his hands.*

> *Thank you, sir. Make I escort you go back house?*

> *No, thank you, I am fine, I can walk home myself, you don try today. I responded with a smile.*

I started my presumed ten-minute walk back home, but unfortunately, this ten-minute walk eventually became half an hour. While on my way, I came across strangers who seemed to recognise me. While some waved with smiles, others came close to exchanging pleasantries.

> *Please excuse me, you must be the son of Mrs Asemota, a strange woman I did not know, probably in her late 50s, asked as she approached me.*

> *Yes, ma'am, I am. I responded.*

> *We heard about the passing of your dearest mother. Your mother was unique—loving and supportive of this community. She evidently left her foot on the sands of time, and we will miss her dearly. May she rest in peace.*

> *Well, thank you ma'am, I really appreciate your condolences, I said with a forged smile as I bowed gently and made my way out of her presence.*

Just when I thought it was all over and I could finally stroll back to my home in peace, at least for today, someone else called out.

The fact that he was asking me a question that he probably knew the answer to was both kind of annoying and weird, but what more could I do in a situation like this?

Yes, but we have stopped production since the eighties. I reminded him.

*Hahaha. Your mother's Swiss bread was our favourite bread then! It was so
delicious, hahaha, he said cheerfully.*

I was in no mood for laughs or small talk, not after what I had just gone through in the banks, and he probably understood my position impulsively from my facial expression.

I want to express my heartfelt condolences to you and your family, he said solemnly.
*Your mother was truly dedicated, loving, and genuine. Her selfless
love is something we can all learn from. I pray God brings
comfort to all of you, especially your father. May her kind soul rest in peace.*

*Thank you for the kind words, sir. I said in appreciation,
I will be on my way now.*

*It is alright. Please send my condolences to your father.
I will,*

I replied and continued my stroll, hoping that would be the last. On my way, I kept thinking of all the condoling words from all these people. It reminded me of my mother and the other promise I made to her on her deathbed—to support and inspire as many as I could. This promise is in conjunction with one of Bob Marley's quotes: "Live for yourself and you will live in vain; live for others, and you will live again."

I finally approached our house entrance and knocked on the gate. Bola came running to open the gate.

Ahhh Stefan, happy to see you again. Welcome back home.

She always called me Stefan, unlike my father, who prefers using my native name.

*Aiiiiii, Bola, thank you. Glad to see that you are looking fresh and well. I
complimented her.*

*We thank God O. How are Thomas and Barbara and your
fabulous wife doing? she asked.*

*They are all fine. I replied as I walked in while she closed the gate behind me.
How is Oga?*

He is in the parlour having tea.

Ahhh!, tea? On this hot afternoon?

*At least he is calm. He asked after you, though, she replied, while laughing at
my earlier remarks.*

As I made my way to the back entrance of our house, which led directly to the sitting room. I found my father sitting on the sofa with his glasses on, reading one of our local newspapers.

Domo, sir, I greeted him with a slight bow.

Osaigbovo, koyo O. You are back?

Yes, sir.

*Welcome. Come have a seat, he responded, pointing to a sofa space close to the
television.*

My father, who is of the Benin ethnicity and a very traditional man, never joked with respect and greetings. He learned this from his own father, who strongly believed that losing one's character means losing everything. He also believed that character, respect, honour and dignity are the elements that make up a well-deserved "greeting" in our culture. In the Benin ethnicity, it is a natural law that the young one must greet the elder first, but this is reversed when the younger one falls sick, and the elder has to greet them first.

*How did it go? he asked as he flipped to the next page of the
newspaper he was reading.*

*It went fine, though stressful. My account is now active, and
I was able to get one of the bank cards working, but I will have
to return in a few days' time for the other card, I replied.*

Hmmm, that's good to hear.

*I met some strangers on my way home, oh.
Strangers?*

Yes. They knew mother when she was alive and spoke very nicely about

As soon as he heard me mention my mother, he started staring hard at the floor beside the sofa, where he was sitting quietly. From all indications, it appeared he was thinking about her.

E H A | 3

It was seven thirty in the morning, and the chirping birds outside my window woke me up. The bright, clear weather hinted that it would be a fantastic day, and I felt so rested.

I lay on my bed gazing at the ceiling, and I couldn't help but notice the movement of the ceiling fan. I guess I was lucky. Most households in my neighbourhood didn't have electricity at this time of day, but the electricity in my home was solar-powered. Hence, the inadequacy of the power distributors in my locality was not an issue. Still, it was appalling how something as basic as electricity was not even stable in a country acclaimed to be Africa's largest economy. In fact, it is even sad to think that the political class could enjoy an uninterrupted power supply in their various residential homes while those they claim to serve languish in darkness with rationed electricity.

I rolled out of bed and stood up to stretch myself. I had plans later today at my father's factory for the mahogany floor Peter and I had to work on. I walked over to the window, looked out, and saw the sun shining it's warm golden light. I stood there for a bit, gazing and observing my slightly busy neighbourhood before stepping out into the hallway to join my father in his room. "He should be up by now," I thought to myself.

Lagiesan, sir! Are you up? I asked as I knocked on his door gently.

Halfway there, he replied with a fully awake tone, which was confusing for me because there's nothing like being half awake.

I don't understand?

Come in, Osaigbovo, and stop shouting. I'm not deaf!

I opened his door and walked in, finding him sitting on his bed, reading the morning newspaper. It seemed he had been awake for a while.

*Lagiesan, I greeted again, in our local dialect, while prostrating
with a slight bow.*

E! Koyo, he replied while still engaged with the newspaper he was reading.

How was your night?

He responded by stretching his right palm at me, showing that I wait a few minutes for him to wrap up what he was reading. He had a serious expression; something in that paper was bothering him. While patiently waiting, I watched him flip the last page of the section he was reading and hand it over to me.

Have you read that article? he asked, pointing at the section he wanted me to review.

No, sir.

Just read it now. This country is in a mess, and if we are not careful, it will get worse.

The article was about how the Nigerian government, in a bid to reduce power theft in our country and increase power production, was budgeting billions of taxpayer funds to construct more power plants across Nigeria. First, while this might seem like good news to anyone not familiar with how corrupt Nigerian politicians are, the opposite is actually the case. In the last 2 decades, we keep hearing that the government has put plans in motion to construct nuclear power plants that will make the issue of rationed electricity a thing of the past. Yet, up till this very moment, the condition of our power supply has even further deteriorated. Over the last 20 years, the same recycled group of politicians has repeatedly stolen public funds and abandoned projects they promised to handle if elected. Seeing the large amount of taxpayers' money that they now claim will be the budget for the so-called power plants, it was clear that they were plotting to steal every penny and milk the country dry.

Can't you see how these people keep deceiving us?

*Yes oh, they are thieves and armed robbers sitting in their air-
conditioned offices, I replied.*

*That's why Malcolm X describes them as house slaves, mtcheew, he hissed
as he stood from his bed to use the bathroom.*

After reading that article, I understood why my father was furious. Malcolm X once delivered a speech about the difference between a "field slave" and a "house slave" during the era of slavery in America.

According to Brother Malcolm, a "house slave" worked inside the master's house as a domestic servant and dearly "loved his master more than he loved himself." Sir Malcolm contrasted this with the field slaves, the masses of the slave population. These slaves never got the benefits of living in the master's house—the food, clothes, shelter, and feeling of superiority—and they were infinitely more bitter about their plight than the house slaves. As he would put it, "If the master's house caught on fire, the house slave would fight harder to put the blaze out than the master would. While on the field, the other slaves would pray for a breeze to pick up."

A good example of this narrative would be the incident that transpired on the 20th of October 2020. While Nigeria (or some part of it) was in flames, the End-SARS (Anti-Robbery Squad) protesters prayed for a breeze, and it happened. These protesters were tired of police crimes and brutality and were prepared to sacrifice anything (even their lives) to make their voices heard. The protest was going on in all major cities around the country, but was more serious in Lagos, the former capital of Nigeria. Our house slaves (corrupt politicians) were terrified by the sights they were seeing. They took a step further to show their cruelty by ordering uniformed army men to open fire on a crowd of around one thousand protesters at the Lekki Toll Gate, leading to the death and severe injury of dozens of people.

The End-SARS protest was a decentralised social movement against police brutality in Nigeria. Before the protest, I used to believe that we Nigerians would rather be docile masses than active citizens, but things changed on the 20th of October. A large part of the people strived to be citizens. Everyone who took part in that protest wanted the right to self-determination, liberty, freedom of movement, privacy, freedom of thought, freedom of religion, freedom of expression, and the right to due process of law.

These were our rights as citizens of Nigeria, and at this point we were fed up and had to refuse the inapplicability that the political ruling class continued to impose on us.

Many people might have been scared to take part in that protest at first, but truth be heard, our Nigerian roads are more dangerous than the bloodshed we saw in that protest. Our hospitals are even scarier than the unprofessionalism we saw that day (the 20th of October) from our so-called "uniformed men."

In fact, engaging with the Nigerian police just by driving towards a checkpoint may have brought a worse outcome than that, yet we were never afraid to go out to protest (despite knowing how ruthless our government was). Why? Because Nigerians understood, we could lose our lives at any moment with the dozens of failed systems we had around us. We have no reliable healthcare system, no improved school curriculum (in fact, no suitable school structures to begin with), no quality fire service, and no reliable and merit-based civil service. Nothing!

I mean, let's remember the pipeline that exploded beside the Bethlehem Girls' College in the middle of a residential area in Lagos on the 15th of March 2020, killing 23 people. How many of these late souls knew they were going to lose their lives that day from a pipeline that belonged to the Nigerian National Petroleum Corporation (NNPC), a pipeline they've refused to maintain for decades?

So if incidents like this, which can be prevented by a government that swore to protect Nigerians, could happen, what more could they do to scare us from protesting? Nothing! Our minds were made up. We had seen enough, heard enough, and suffered enough. These and several other factors motivated the End-SARS protest.

Unfortunately, because of that very protest, we were able to see firsthand how brutal and heartless our political class was. To make matters worse, the suspected politician who reportedly ordered the massacre of young Nigerians on the 20th of October 2020 would later be the President. Who could have imagined that? I guess no one would.

But what more would you have expected of "house slaves" ruling over a geographic area that was never meant to be? Archaeological research has proven that people lived in various parts of what is now known as Nigeria for thousands of years before the British came. Different empires and kingdoms, including the Songhai (which peaked in the 15th-16th centuries), the Benin Empire, the Oyo Empire, and various Hausa states, flourished in parts of this region over the centuries. The land and its diverse cultures had a rich history that long predates Nigeria's now corrupt and poverty-ridden nation-state, created by the British in 1914.

The colonial era started after the British annexation of Lagos in 1861, and a legislative and executive council were constituted for it. Sir Hugh Clifford drafted the first Nigerian Constitution, which was then changed over the years. Other colonial lackeys, like Charles Cameron and Bernard Bourdillon, played their parts in marginalising Nigeria for administrative purposes. Even the name "Nigeria" is a colonial name bequeathed by the colonial ruler, Lord Lugard.

During the period that led up to 1960, the elite Nigerian politicians selected as "house slaves" were told to shut up, listen, and follow. Locals like Dr Kalu Ezera, who first suggested in 1960, that Nigeria's name be changed to the United Republic of Songhai, got ignored by reactionary colonial lackeys who formed the core of Nigeria's early "nationalists." Dr Kalu Ezera was a foresighted and wise political scientist.

Nigeria, as we see today, is ruled by these "house slaves" and people with NO VISION. Hence why they can carry out the most unimaginable crimes against those they swore to protect. These so-called leaders have been planted in their various positions since 1960, and all they do is pass the relay baton to the next s-elected house slave to continue the damage.

It is my firm belief that Nigeria's unity must be renegotiated because we were brought together by Lord Lugard and British colonialism without any mandate from our people. This strange relationship of "house and field slave" was permanently hammered into existence by our so-called independence in 1960.

The rest of us, who are just law-abiding citizens with no political power or positions, can be described in this hypothetical narrative as mere "field slaves." Field slaves can be very loyal. They accept the conditions they are put into: they drive on bad roads, they can live without basic amenities and do not complain, and they will stay in darkness without electricity. While they get taxed for all these basic amenities, they are yet to enjoy them.

Over 20% of our primary school children cannot read and write even after completing the so-called "basic education" offered by the government because of poor teaching and learning facilities, not to mention the poorly trained teachers employed by the same corrupt government. Their parents are illiterate anyway, so they accept their children's situation and keep quiet about it. This is the "field slave" mentality we must fight against.

In the past 20 years, there has been a claim that the Nigerian government "banned" history from the national curriculum. This has become a hackneyed refrain. It's often uttered in moments of glaring display of historical ignorance, especially by young people. But this refrain is both dishonest and inaccurate. History was never a mandatory subject at any point in Nigeria's history. My 17-year-old son knows more about Swiss history than most Nigerian university graduates know about Nigerian history.

The End-SARS protest might have been the start of a series of continued struggles to redefine Nigeria, and I applaud every person who took part in a non-violent way. Certain people went beyond bounds by damaging public property, which should be condemned. Although we all have the right to protest, it would be foolish to say we should express our grievances by unlawful means. We cannot use illegality and violence to fix brutality like our politicians.
In the meantime, while politicians have used tribalism and cultural differences to evangelise hate and disunity among Nigerians, Yusuf Buhari, son of Nigeria's former President Muhammadu Buhari, and bride Zahra Bayero, got married in 2021. Their marriage attracted people from all walks of life, even "respectable" Nigerian politicians such as Goodluck Ebele Jonathan and Atiku Abubakar. Several PDP (Peoples Democratic Party) governors and national assembly members were seen wining and dining with opposition party members, the APC (All Progressives Congress), as if they all belonged to one big happy family.

Yusuf's marriage reminded me of a scene in the film "Django Unchained." House slaves will always reconcile with other house slaves while they manipulate the field slaves to hate themselves, and their children will always be able to marry each other. However, a house slave can never be reconciled with a field slave. There will always be friction between them. The position of the house slaves on the plantation served to divert many blacks from questioning their treatment and attempting to fight it. Being a house slave meant security and entitlement to the black owner, creating an environment where slaves yearned for a higher position in the slave system rather than pondering ways to fight the system itself.

From my understanding, house slaves were deliberately put in such ambiguous positions. At work, it is the principle of "divide et impera". Household slaves were, indeed, much closer to their masters than field slaves. This could actually pose a threat, as these slaves were aware of their lifestyle, and with a revolt, they might have been a wonderful source of information for the rebels. However, despite being the same slaves deprived of any individual rights, household slaves were very reluctant to show any support to their field colleagues.

To whom do our house slave presidents and corrupt political leaders answer? Yet, Ibrahim Babangida, Buhari, and Obasanjo, just to name a few, have committed documented atrocities and are among the wealthiest African politicians. They remain untouched and still maintain their status quo. We have seen what happened to the likes of Saddam Hussein, Che Guevara, or Gaddafi when they were no longer willing to maintain their status quo. They were killed by Western forces!
In most cases, after the "damage has been done," these western powers and companies would provide controversial compensation to the countries or families left behind. As in the case of Ken Saro-Wiwa, Shell PLC paid over 15 million dollars to the families of the executed activists to improve their imagery.

We Nigerians should not expect any person or political party to change the situation in our beloved country. Change comes from within oneself, and without creating a new ideology in ourselves and using it to form a new political party, there's little to no hope of changing this country for good. We must not depend on any old political party or corrupt candidates representing them.

This won't work. Why? The manifestos of old political parties are designed to maintain the status quo of our current situation. Today, 30% to 45% of the Nigerian population is illiterate. Democracy cannot work when over 30% of the population can't even read to understand the country's political structure and setup.

After a few hours of deliberating on societal issues, I left my father in Bola's care and headed straight to our factory to join Peter so we could process the mahogany floor together. Arriving at the factory, I walked past my mother's old office, and memories of her popped up. These memories were so strong that I had to step into the office. I strolled to her window and flipped the light grey curtain open. The dust that erupted from it almost made me lose my breath. I stared through the window and saw the weather changing rapidly. In seconds, everywhere was dark, and thunderstorms were erupting. It was barely half-eight, and it seemed clear it was about to rain heavily.

"Oga Stefan, mahogany has been prepared and is awaiting your inspection," Peter announced as he approached with a Chinese-made electric or solar lantern. He had probably been looking for me everywhere and finally found me in my mother's office. I was so hypnotised by my thoughts while staring through the window that I couldn't comprehend what was just said. Instead, I reset my gaze on the lantern he was holding in astonishment, and my thoughts instantly transitioned into observation.

I carefully examined this object but found little or no difference from my father's crude kerosene lamps in the 80s, which were manufactured in the East of Nigeria. If the manufacturing era had continued to this present time, those crudely manufactured items of the past by Awka Smiths could have been refined into admirable consumer commodities.

This is why I have always admired the cleverness of the Chinese, who have now dominated the Nigerian markets in all ramifications. It is no exaggeration to say that there is no Nigerian home without Chinese items, be it kitchen appliances, electronic equipment, or even furniture. China has totally replaced Britain and Japan as Nigeria's exporter of consumer goods. What China does is she takes our primary goods and sell us manufactured ones. This was also the essence of colonialism (another form of imperialism).

Peter helped me out of my deep reflection by giving me a solid push on my shoulder.

Oga Stefan?

Ahh Peter, sorry, what were you saying?

I hope you're okay, sir?

I'm fine Peter. So where were we?

Today's agenda, sir, the mahogany has been prepared and is awaiting your inspection in the machine section, he replied.

Okay, let's go check it out together.

On arrival, I noticed that Peter and Ayo had pre-cut, planned, and grooved 200 pieces of flooring parquet in less than two hours!

Wow. Guys, well done. I see you have been busy. You must have started early, I complimented.

Yes, sir, we had dried mahogany wood in stock, Peter informed me.

I picked up one piece of the prepared plank to verify the tongue and groove, but I noticed they were not smooth. This was probably a result of the blunt profiling knives used.

Not bad. I see you have not done the final sanding yet, I said.

Yes, sir, our sanding machine is down. We informed Oga a long time ago; he must have forgotten, Ayo replied.

Are you serious?

Yes sir, even our trucks are also down for months now. No spare parts were found to fix them.

*Chai! So, what are our options now, Ayo? Where can we sand 200
pieces of planks here in Benin?*

*Well, I know a place around Stadium Road, but we might have to
rent a taxi.*

*Okay, what other issues are pending here in the factory? I asked as I turned my
head around the machine section.*

Ayo rushed into one office in the hallway and came out with what seemed like a sheet of
paper.

*Here is a list I made some months back. It was adapted from an
existing list Benson made long ago. I have tried updating the items
regularly, he said as he handed me a worn-out foolscap paper.*

Thanks! I will see what can be done here within the week.

Alright sir.

The first time I noticed organisational chaos in the factory was in 2013 when I visited.
Then, my mother told me she hadn't been to the factory in over a month. I asked her
why, but I got no response. Since then, things have been falling apart, and my father has
been struggling to manage them. Reflecting on the 2013 period, I would say that was
when my mother's illness started, and things only just got worse… slowly.

*Ayo, please can you contact your person at Stadium Road now to
set up a meet-up this afternoon? I am hoping it shouldn't take us
more than half a day to sand these 200 pieces so we can start
fixing them at the house tomorrow.*

Alright, let me put a call across now.

Within a few minutes, while I was observing the planks for possible wood bugs, Ayo
walked up to me.

Boss, I'm done with the call.

What did they say? I asked curiously.

They said okay, and won't charge us.

Why?

Because their boss knows Oga, he explained to me.

Oh! Okay, that's great! I said.

All the planks were stapled to a piece of crate. We started re-selecting the planks for holes, uneven rings, and other possible wood bugs. Out of 200 pieces, we could only keep 175 planks. After lunch, we loaded these planks onto the pickup van Peter organised and headed to Stadium Road.

Arriving at the entrance gate of the furniture factory, the driver honked at the gate. The security personnel came out and approached our car to verify our contact credentials.

He then opened the gate, and we drove through. The foreman, Aimua, welcomed us and showed us around the place. The factory was big, spacious, and well-equipped, like ours. From the outside, anyone would think it was a secondary school. However, the machinery setup/positioning was very chaotic, and badly arranged.

The workers at the factory were, in the course of their work, exposed to several hazards that put them at risk of severe debilitating health conditions. They, however, seemed not to care much about such dangers, and I think they've never attended a class or received any training on workplace safety.

Most of them were walking barefoot and without masks, while some were wearing the wrong shoes. Plus, the factory had no sawdust extractor, so workers were inhaling the constant dust extracted from the various machines, such as the wide-band sanding machine we were supposed to use for our planks.

In addition, the factory was in a state of disarray, with wood pieces scattered across the floor. Without proper caution, this situation could easily result in tripping and pose a potential workplace hazard. My interaction with the foreman and carpenters revealed the director knew their potential difficulties and challenges, but has provided no solutions yet.

I became baffled again about how my mother set up our factory in Benin City. Cleanliness, safety, order, and a working mentality were integrated into the daily process. Just last year (2019), during my trip to Nigeria, I visited the foreman who had been in charge of our factory for about 15 years. Benson was his name. He opened his own workshop, and I was happy and proud to see traits of my mother's influence.

Anyway, back to the primary matter at hand. Aimua ordered his apprentices to bring the planks out of the pickup van. As they assembled the planks before the wide-band Sanding machine, he fired up the machine, gauged the expected plank thickness and ran a sample. In no time, all the planks were sanded, and the same apprentices helped us load them back into the pickup van. We showed our gratitude and drove off.

As I sat in the back and watched the Ogbe Stadium fly by us, I imagined the stress we would have avoided if our sanding machine had been still working. The machine stopped working about 32 years ago. Back then, we were the only ones that had such a machine in Benin City and maybe Nigeria, I would say.

However, we had no local technicians who could repair the machine, and the cost of engaging an expatriate was exuberant. This machine we used today was new (just slightly over a year old), and the foreman told me they needed a technician to maintain it. Hence, most of these machines will be rundown within the next 5 years because of the same problems we faced. If only there were skilled Nigerian technicians who could handle machines like these, but again, these machines are scarce, and only a few furniture factories in Nigeria have them, it would not be a lucrative skill for any artisan.

E N Ẹ | 4

It was six o'clock in the morning, and I watched calmly as my father nodded his head at the words of my uncle, the eldest of the Asemotas. As we prepared to bury my mother, he was here to advise the family on how to go about it the right way and under Benin culture.

One of the biggest life events in Nigeria is a funeral. Funerals are celebrated or mourned, and in my mother's case, the family feared that if all burial customs weren't followed, Klara Asemota wouldn't transcend to become an ancestor and would haunt the living instead. Scary, right? Well, that's one of the many beliefs of the Benin culture for funerals.

Benins believe their deceased family members become ancestors when they die. This is a little weird, you would imagine, but it's been a norm in our culture for centuries. It's believed that our parents, siblings, and close relatives are our guardian angels after death, and for this reason, their burial rites and ceremonies must be done as our tradition demands; otherwise, their souls will never be at peace.

This culture is not just limited to the Benins; in almost every part of the country, you would discover that no expense is spared to plan a Nigerian burial. Be it lavish meals, dancing pallbearers, or even animal sacrifices, all are done in a show-off fashion. Funerals are so important here in Nigeria that families save up for their loved one's burial instead of medical expenses. It's a sick behaviour that has grown to become a norm in Nigerian society.

As part of the burial plans, my father gave me a handful of tasks to execute, including renovating the family sitting and dining rooms. Work was supposed to begin later today, but my uncle was here to plan a consultation visit with our family to the Esama of Benin, so plans had to change. We needed guidance from a palace chief on how to proceed with my mother's burial rites, and the Esama was the best cultural custodian to consult with.

A couple of days later, I was sitting with my father and the eldest of the Asemota family members in the corner of the vast waiting lounge at the Esama of Benin's home, glued to our chairs, nervously waiting for an audience. The intimidating ambience was a sight to behold. Everything around us was cast in gold; the door handles, the rails, and the seats.

My grandfather's role as a sword bearer to Oba Akenzua II of Benin helped integrate our family into His Highness's tight circle. His relationship with the Oba of Benin grew into a fruitful and faithful friendship that extended through the reign of Oba Akenzua II's son, Oba Erediauwa.

Still wiggling our legs and waiting, I asked my father,

> *What is the Esama title exactly, and how can I have it?*

My father laughed and then replied:

> *Osaigbovo... The title 'Esama' traditionally means 'Son of the People.' The Oba of Benin created this chieftaincy role decades ago so that the Esama could act as a communicator and 'middle man' between the Oba and us, the Benins.*
>
> *Okay, what kind of responsibility does the title hold?*
>
> *Hmm, it's majorly around diplomacy and assisting the Benins in medial, monetary, and any other form of private venture. He replied.*

I stared at him for some time and asked,

> *But Father, why are we here exactly? Why can't we just handle the burial in a normal way? Why go through all these rites?*

He understood what I meant because we had been waiting for the Esama for over an hour, so he tried to explain the situation to me as best he could.

> *I understand what you mean, Osaigbovo, but it's complex. On one hand, we have a privileged relationship with the Oba that we have to maintain. On the other hand, our responsibilities are tied to this privilege. The Edo burial rites are part of these responsibilities, so we must include them in our plans as we bury your mother. It's not even debatable. He explained.*

Still observing the curiosity in my eyes, he continued,

> *The last time I was here was in 1976, when I was opportune enough to have an audience with Oba Erediauwa. His Highness*

*emphasised the importance of having a traditional burial
according to the Benin rites. I have now grown to understand why
this is important, and I hope you do, too. You see, my son, the
endlessly leaping flames of westernisation have continued to
engulf us and all that we are. But all that we are is rooted deep in
our customs and traditions, and without them, we are nothing.
Your grandfather was a true embodiment of the Benin culture
and the traditions of our people, and I must follow in his
footsteps. He concluded, tapping me on the lap.
Do you understand me?*

Although I still had some questions, I had to play safe to avoid another series of lectures, so I nodded in acceptance, hoping that would do the magic. Unfortunately, it didn't.

*Prior to your mother's visit to Benin City in 1967, he continued,
just before we got married, your grandfather took us to the
Oba's Palace, where we received the blessings of Oba Erediauwa,
and your mother was fully accepted as…*

Are the Asemotas here? a steward asked, interrupting my father.

My uncle signalled to him we were present. He then requested we follow him from the outer lounge to the sitting room. Another steward immediately approached us to inquire about our choice of drinks. My father and uncle replied with cold water. I felt like cooling off with a cold beer, but I didn't know what made up the pre-trials, assuming I was being tested for honourable conduct. I shouldn't start so early to destroy the impression of "a wonderful son." So I hesitated and told the steward: "Malt will be okay."

After a while, Lady Cherry entered with her husband (the Esama). His special seat (or throne) in the outlay was unmistakable. It was made of bronze, and you could feel the ambience of royalty from your seat.

He stared at me for God knows how long while I sipped my glass of malt. I did not pay attention at first, but as the stare got weirder, I felt he was wondering what I was doing in that meeting, because I was the youngest person in the room.
My heart was beating fast as I occasionally stared back at him and looked away. Luckily for me, Lady Cherry came to my rescue.

*Ehen, chief, here is the son of Adun Asemota, a sword bearer of
Oba Akenzua II, she announced to him.*

His countenance returned to a friendly mode, and when his voice came, it was soothing.

Welcome. I remember your father. He passed away in 1976, right?.

What followed was more of a monologue with my father, so I resisted getting involved in their discussion and occasionally nodded when I observed my father doing so. With the staring contest I just survived, I was determined not to overreact or do what is popularly known here in Nigeria as "over-sabi." The truth was, I just wanted to go home.

The conversation lasted an eternity. Lady Cherry, who had gone inside for some business, re-entered to announce that lunch was ready. The chief grabbed my father's hand, and my father pulled my uncles and me along to the dining section. There is no point describing the lunch; it was the best of African and continental dishes. For the first time since entering the chief's home, I became less artificial and acted my true self. I did justice to the Pounded Yam and Egusi soup we were served while listening to the discussion between the chief and my father.

Our visit was to inform the Esama of Benin about my mother's passing. I listened as my father received advice from the chief about how to conduct the burial proceedings. I couldn't stop thinking about one of his remarks.

"In Benin, there is little value attached to individualism," he said as he looked around to see how concentrated everyone was. "Or, a self-sustaining, independent self," he continued. "The Edo culture defined, tested, and proved itself for thousands of years as the basis of natural adaptation, living, social growth, and cohesiveness in the human environment," he said. "It is an African-proven way of life in pure conformity with the formation of the natural systems of the universe, and we must all respect it." He concluded.
I believe he was right. My mother lived in Benin City for almost half a century. In 1967, she was welcomed and accepted as a White Edo woman who loved our culture. Hence, her burial must show these cultural attributes, as the Esama suggested.

After concluding our consultations with him, we bid farewell and continued our journey home. While in the car, I quickly called Peter to inform him we would be installing the Mahogany flooring planks and requested that he bring 2 apprentices while coming. We were supposed to fix it a few days back, but my uncle's visit changed everything.

We arrived home just shortly after ten o'clock. My father was tired and decided to retire to his room upstairs. I made my way directly to the dining room. Since we had already removed all the furniture earlier in the week, I began removing the baseboards around the room. It takes some strength and finesse to leave them intact. Prying the boards away from the wall took me about thirty minutes. I worked a small section at a time and loosened the length of the baseboard instead of trying to leverage the entire board from one side. I learned these little tricks as a carpenter.

The trick to removing the parquet floor is all about the adhesive that keeps the tiles in place. However, since these parquet tiles in our dining room were laid using the floating technique (without adhesive glue to the floor), all I needed to do was grab a crowbar and begin removing the tiles gradually.

It took me about an hour to remove all the wooden tiles and clean the dining room with a broom.

Peter called to let me know he would arrive soon so we could install the mahogany floor together. Not only is my father a big fan of this wood, but because of the timber shortage, it's also the only suitable wood you can buy in Benin City.

Although timber is a renewable resource, it's not entirely sustainable. If forests are being harvested quicker than they are being replenished, which is the situation in Edo State, then there's a real possibility of shortage. The implications are far-reaching, with WWF's "Living Forests" report series concluding that global demand for timber is expected to triple by 2050 due to increased demand for wood and paper products from growing economies and populations. This report's analysis shows that Nigeria only has 11 years of timber forest. This report further states that the primary forest is being depleted at an alarming rate, with the most extreme example being Nigeria, which is losing 99% of its natural forests. It is crazy when you imagine the tremendous impact on biodiversity and other important forest ecosystem functions.

Timber in construction, whilst innovative, is nothing new. Societies worldwide have used trees and their derivative products for thousands of years. It's clear to see why—there is ample global supply for the foreseeable future, making it a sustainable and responsible product to build with. These days, timber has been honed, crafted, and divided into many areas to offer a multitude of options for the budding specifier. Modern timber offers a host of economic and logistical benefits for the offsite and modular construction sectors, as it is largely factory-prepared and brought to the site for rapid assembly. But only if we use it ethically; otherwise, we can only expect shortages to get worse.

As I was sweeping, Bola met me in the dining room.

Stefan, the food is ready, oh. Do you want to eat it now?

Ahh Bola, I am blessed. Thank you very much. Yes, I would.

Great! I will serve the black soup on the kitchen table, she said as she made her way back to the kitchen.

I was excited that she cooked black soup. It's been a while since I ate this dish, and to be frank, Bola is such a wonderful cook that I miss her meals anytime I am overseas.

The black soup is nothing like the ancient Spartan soup made of boiled pigs' legs, blood, salt, and vinegar. It's a delicious meal you'd relish; in fact, I dare say that Black Soup is Nigeria's most popular Edo food. The black soup, locally called "Omoebe soup," is a tasty meal made from local herbs and spices. The soup derives its name from the colour it takes on, which results from using bitter leaf and Effirin (Scent Leaf) vegetables. When these vegetables are ground, they produce a deep, dark colour. Additionally, the soup is made with banga sauce (palm fruit sauce) instead of palm oil, which also adds to its dark colour. The black soup is as nutritious as it is tasty. The herbs used are quite therapeutic and a good option for those on a diet, as they can help reduce calories. This soup is best served with pounded yam, eba, or starch. On this occasion, Bola served it with eba. I made my way to the kitchen to join Bola for lunch. We sat at a round Mansonia wooden table, chatting and eating.

As we were about to finish lunch, Peter and the apprentice arrived through the front door, sweating.

Aah, Peter. Welcome.

Thank you, sir.

Hope all is good? This one, you are sweating like this.

Na our motor spoil for road oh, so we just gat trek am come.

Aiiiii, sorry. Sit down, make I go bring cold water for una, I offered as I left the meal I was eating to get them some cold water to drink.

Much appreciated, sir, he responded graciously.

After hours of fixing the new mahogany wood floor, I gave Peter and the apprentice who assisted us some money to use for transport and personal upkeep and thanked them for their help. They offered to help with the cleanup, but I told them not to worry; I would handle it myself. As I was inspecting the work we did, my father joined me downstairs. He had just woken up from his nap.

Wow, this is nice!

Aaah, you've woken up?

Yes. Where is Peter?

He just left not too long ago.

Okay. Osaigbovo, please come. I want to discuss something with you, he said, walking to the living room.

I followed behind him, trying to figure out what the topic was. We sat down, and I asked if he would like to have his dinner now.

No. I will eat later.

Alright. So, what do you want to discuss?

I think it is best we bury your mother in Switzerland.

Why?

You know we are at the peak of COVID-19, he said, staring at me.

Okay?

*Evidently, Osaigbovo, the proportion of diasporans being buried
abroad has been increasing exponentially.*

Yes, that is true. I agreed.

*The reality now, my son, is that the burial here will be far more
expensive considering the cost of repatriation for your mother, the
cost of burial, and the cost of multiple family trips to attend the
funeral, memorial, and tombstone ceremony, among others.*

He stopped to hear if I had anything to say, but I remained quiet because his points
were valid. So he continued.

*This is even worsened by the bills that may arise from prolonged
funeral vigils because of delayed burials. So, my son, I firmly
suggest that your mother be buried in Switzerland. Or, what do you think?*

It was a lot to process, but he made valid points.

*We will have to first discuss it with Barbara and Thomas, too, and
see what they think, I suggested.*

I have done that this evening, and they think it's a good idea.

Then it's fine by me, father. Let's talk more about it tomorrow.

I was already feeling a headache and needed to shower and relax. Plus, I had a busy
schedule the next day, so I needed some sleep.

Good night, sir. I greeted as I made my way to the bedroom.

Good night! He replied.

I removed my clothes and jumped into the shower as soon as I got to my room. During
my bath, I thought about everything he said and wondered why we even visited the
Esama. At least I understood why my father was asking for my mother's burial to be
done in Switzerland, but how would his brothers (my uncles) take the news? Well, they
will figure that out, eventually. I changed into my pyjamas and lay on my bed, staring at
the ceiling, and slowly drifted off asleep.

I S Ẹ N | 5

It was eleven o'clock in Benin, and the weather was hot. The temperatures were so high that even the ceiling fan in my room offered about as much relief as a whisper in a thunderstorm.

The West African heat is quite unlike the southern European heat; it is unrelenting, sticky, and can make you lose more sweat than any average exercise. I was on the bed baking in sweat, staring at the ceiling and trying to arrange my itinerary for the day when my phone rang. It was my sister, Barbara.

> *Steffi! How are you doing?*

> *I'm okay, and you?*

> *Well, I'm good. How's father? Hope he's taking his medications?*

> *Yeah, he's fine, I replied.*

> *Oh! Okay, Hmmm. I wanted to tell you to remember my hairbrush when coming. Please add it to your bag now.*

When Barbara mentioned the hairbrush, I had a flashback to the 80s, when she would always try to tame her slightly unusual, wavy, but not quite kinky hair back in order before leaving for secondary school in the morning. Back then, her school required this mode of hair tradition, and our mother would usually come running into the bathroom to aid her in speeding up the process. As a seven-year-old boy back then, I found such "bathroom mornings before school" unforgettable.

> *Alright, I will do that now before I head out.*

> *Oh. You're going out?*

As a young boy in the 60s, I loved visiting our neighbourhood barbershop. Looking back, I understand now that barbers do more than just cut hair – they help shape identities. They are also influential because their shops are what I call "public intimate spaces". People share their problems in conversation with the barber. The barbers learn from their stories and share this knowledge with other customers. So, barbershops are not only a place for cutting hair but also a space where people meet, relax and discuss issues, build relationships, seal business deals, and even address intimate subjects.

In the 60s, my favourite barber was "Fin-boy." His shop was one of the best in our area then, and Fin-boy had a fabulous hair sign in front of it. This signboard was hand-drawn and featured many of the hairstyles he could do (the most popular haircuts were "Professor," "Girls Follow Me," "Carl Lewis," and "School Boi). Many of these hairstyles were quite similar and mostly inspired by football stars, African artists, or icons in Nigeria. While the hairstyles themselves overlapped, their functions differed depending on the city.
What I liked about Fin-Boy's shop were the chairs, each with a large mirror in front of it. Most of the mirrors were shattered, yet functional. Another thing I liked was the cool background music playing at his shop whenever I was having a cut, usually the newest Afrobeat or African highlife from the great Fela Aníkúlápó Kuti. Fridays, I believe, were Fin-boy's romantic days, when he only played Celine Dion songs. At his barbershop, both men and women came in to have their hair trimmed, and it was exciting for me to be in their presence, listening to their different life experiences and stories. At times, there would be debates between male and female customers on intimate topics; at other times, it would be an elderly man educating everyone on the proper herbal remedies used to make natural hair look darker.

When you remember those days and how the men and women were so proud of their natural hair and compare them now to this "woke" generation that believes entirely in artificiality, it's easy to see how the world has changed, which in terms of morality, I wouldn't say for good.

My grandma, aunties, and teachers all had natural short hair and were proud of it. But what is this 'natural hair' I'm talking about? Well, in an African context, when one's hair is not processed, dyed, bleached, straightened or otherwise chemically altered to conform to Eurocentric standards, it is called natural. For my grandmother, to maintain her God-given natural hair, she and other girls in her family would have their hairs braided, and it was not just a matter of choice. It was a tradition they had to adhere to.

Once a month, she and her sisters would be sent to their relatives and return home with a fresh bed of locks, cornrows, or twists tightly wound and weaved to the top of their heads. Hair braiding is a process that takes an average of five to six hours per head, so you can imagine the patience they had to have. Not only does this skill demand physicality and patience, but it also brings to light what these hairstyles mean to black women and how braiding can forge and empower a black community.

Now, fast forward to the present day. When I see black ladies wearing wigs and stretched or permed hair, I find their new senses of "wokeism" and artificiality as a lack of awareness. On a few occasions when I've been privileged to discuss with these ladies, I would bring up the topic to see their reactions and understand their reasons. Some people assume that asking a lady about her hairstyle is equivalent to peeking inside her handbag. Still, with the way I introduce the issue, they feel comfortable discussing it.

It might interest you to know that black women who straighten their natural hair are generally seen to be practising self-hatred, according to both academic studies and popular culture (Banks, 2000; Thompson, 2009). Hair straightening is thought to be "indicative of a dislike of black physical attributes and an emulation of white physical characteristics." To put it in simpler terms, black women change their naturally "kinky" or "nappy" hair to seem white and remove themselves from their African origin. But I tend to think otherwise.

Despite what these so-called "researches and popular culture" claim, I believe that every woman's primary aim is to be attractive and presentable at any cost, and this applies to women of all races, black and white. It's worth noting that hair volume extensions are one of the newest trends among the top cosmetic surgery procedures performed by white women, varying from Lip implants made of silicone, Buttock augmentation, Hip, upper-outer-buttock, outer thigh, Hip flank to Volume hair extensions. I could also say that white women alter their natural "traits" because they want to distance themselves from their Caucasian heritage.

Reviewing these cosmetic surgeries mentioned above, I would say that most white women want to look like black women and vice versa. So, there isn't any use in classifying women based on their appearances, since they all want the best for themselves. Though "looking white" is often the assumed motivation, there are many more factors that play into a black woman's decision to straighten her hair.

To dismiss all hair straightening practices as self-hatred is an over-simplification that fails to consider historical context and culturally embedded motivations. Some factors, such as media advertisements, slavery, and internalisation of white beauty standards, must be addressed in order to gain a more complete understanding of the prevalence of hair alteration practices among Black women and body trait alteration practices among Caucasian women. I would like to shed more light on the aspect of slavery.

First, let's look at Mrs Michelle Obama as an example. Styles representing the European aesthetic are more accepted and less likely to upset the global beauty mainstream. However, African-inspired hairstyles are given different attention. To call someone a nappy head is an insult, and the word "nappy," which simply refers to the kinky nature of hair, is nearly a swear word. The term is euphemistically referred to as "natural" in polite contexts. What if Mrs Obama wore her hair in cornrows or wore it similar to Afeni Shakur, Nikki Giovanni, Barbara Jordan, or Eleanor Norton? Would she have been able to maintain her sophisticated and near-perfect image?

Natural hair wearers have seen their politics, patriotism, and even their hygiene come under attack. Their Afros, braids, locks, and twists have been considered unprofessional, and some who have prided themselves in these hairstyles have either been demoted or lost their jobs. Wearers of natural hairstyles also have not escaped being labelled as subversive or perceived as social misfits.

Slavery, racism, and white supremacy have had lasting adverse effects on black identity. The devaluation of African physical features, including hair, came because of being thrust into a cultural context where blackness exists as the antithesis of beauty. As a result, many blacks developed a colour complex, representing an intragroup preference for features that minimise African ancestry.

The implication of the colour hierarchy imposed on slaves has been the collective restructuring of black beauty ideals to parallel white ideals, which do not include African-like features. Despite white beauty being unattainable for black women, hair straightening techniques remain popular because they represent a chance to get closer to the ideal. Since neither the texture nor the length of natural black hair conforms to the traditional picture of beauty, black women have had to take culturally depreciating measures to come close to the dominant standards.

Women wearing wigs remind me of the Tignon Law in the 1700s, which forced black women in Louisiana to wear wraps because their beautiful, ornate hairstyles were considered a threat to the status quo. So, where are we now in Africa? In the centuries since, we've seen the abolition of slavery and the Civil Rights Movement in America. But have things changed for black women's hair globally? Still today, the act of not manipulating hair is perceived as radical to a certain extent. Natural hair still catches many people off guard in countries outside of Africa. It fascinates them.

It is even worse in Nigeria; here, some women have no status if they don't wear wigs produced elsewhere. Wigs are almost like the identity of beauty among Nigerians and women.

It is tough to tell how things turned out this way, but to every kinky-haired girl looking in the mirror, frustrated with what they see, cringing as the comb gets stuck in their coily strands, tempted by the appeal of wigs, remember that history proves the actual reason your hair is considered unruly, and that is because it is beautiful and has the potential to upend white supremacy.

In my opinion, the internalisation of the Black Beauty Movement should be called to life. Hair modification should be used to spark black women's beliefs that it is more about feeling attractive on a personal level than it is about looking white in this movement.

Stefan…, Stefan! Bola called out to me.

Yeah?

Food is ready!

Wow, so quick?

Yes, o! It looks like you have been sleeping.

No, oh. Not really. I was just reflecting on something.

That's alright.

I'll be coming down soon.

Okay.

I gathered enough momentum, snuck out of bed, and went downstairs to the living room. While seated, I stumbled upon the day's Edo Express newspaper beside me. Flipped open the first page to glance at the latest happenings. Unfortunately, just as if my brain was still caught up in my earlier thoughts, the first thing I saw in the newspaper was an advertisement for a wig company.

This company started its operations around 2016, and its objective was to promote the circulation of Nigerian-made wigs, eliminating the high importation cost of wigs and making them available for all women in Nigeria. As I read this advertisement in disgust, Bola calmed my nerves with the aroma of the boiled yam and scrambled eggs she served before me on a stool. I immediately set aside the newspaper to handle business.

After battling this fantastic breakfast dish, I returned to my room to freshen up before heading out. Since my father had left earlier with the car, I was left with one option: taking a taxi to my tennis training at Benin Club before heading to my barbershop for a clean shave.

Barely outside our gate, I jumped on an "okada," which took me to the main junction. I had to cross the road in the opposite direction as my destination was the Government Reserved Area (GRA). Crossing roads in Benin is a life-threatening act because of how unruly the public transport drivers behave; it gets more complicated during the rainy season, and if you're not careful enough to look at both sides of the road when crossing a one-way street, one mad driver may just hit you down and run off. It's that bad.

Fortunately for me, I am experienced with the Naija lifestyle, so I carefully observed both ends of the road before attempting to make a cross and did so with all my bones intact. Once on the other side of the road, I hopped in a chattered yellow Danfo bus with tinted black windows, made my way to the back, and sat down. I gazed at the driver as he manoeuvred through the Ikpoba hill traffic.

I noticed that the cause of the hectic traffic was the Oregbeni market day. This market traditionally occurs every 4 days. It draws buyers from far and wide because of its huge stock of freshly harvested crops, fruits, and vegetables and also its strategic location.

Because of the street trading and the large number of buyers, the market days are often marked by heavy traffic in the Ikpoba Hill area.

Having just passed the Ikpoba River relaying bridge, just by Ewa Road junction, our bus driver was stopped by men dressed in black police attire and wearing police caps. They swung their batons and sticks at the driver, letting him know he should stop the vehicle, and he did, hoping it was some sort of routine police check that was going on.

A black car parked beside the road had more of their comrades in it. Two policemen approached our bus and asked the driver for his papers. He presented the credentials to them. Then they asked to check his boot. He flipped open the boot, but they insisted he come out and follow them to the boot so they could inspect it together. He obliged. Still thinking nothing was wrong. He had only his laptop bag on the bus, anyway. Afterwards, they demanded that everyone step out of the bus for a routine check. Since I was alone on the bus, I stepped out. As they approached me, I noticed they were not really doing body checks. One of them told me to follow them to the police station. I asked why, but they retorted angrily.

Trying not to cause trouble, I obliged. The whole drama got to a point where they asked me to step in their car, and I felt something might be wrong. Still, about 5 or more men were surrounding me. So I sat beside the guy in the front holding a gun while another guy entered their car and sat behind. They told the other guys to follow them in the other black car.

At this point, I knew that these men were up to something. I felt that dreadful, creepy feeling in my spine when I suspected my life was in danger as the driver started the car and drove off.

My brain was injected with adrenaline. What should I do? What must I do? My survival instincts kicked in.

Just as we approached a street where a few people gathered beside a roadside hawker. I knew it was now or never. I grabbed the steering wheel and swung it sharply to the left, ensuring he bashed the oncoming vehicle. I hoped that if I could bash any vehicle, this would be enough to make our car stop; it would also draw attention, and the owner of the bashed car would have to step down and approach us. That quick thinking on my part saved my life. Immediately, our car crashed into the other vehicle, the policeman in the back panicked, leaving behind his baton and face cap; he opened the door and dashed off. The black car following behind sped away without hesitation.

I now had to wrestle with the guy in front. Using all my strength, I choked the guy with my legs wrapped around his neck. A group of men standing by the roadside now came vocally to my rescue as one of them shouted, "Stefan" three times. Hearing my name gave me courage and made me continue, hoping they would join me in my struggles. I looked at the guy I was trying to strangle; to my surprise, he was smiling! I looked back at the group of men to see if they were walking towards our car. But they hadn't moved an inch. Suddenly, I realised I was dreaming.

> *Oga! You don reach where you dey go O, try wake up! the driver yelled out,*
> *trying to wake me up.*

My eyes slowly fluttered open. I glanced at the window but couldn't really see anything, but I could still hear the faint voice from earlier that called my name.

> *Him be dey sleep since? the same voice asked.*

> *Yes, oh.*

> *Nor worry, I go wake am now.*

I felt a firm hand tapping me on the shoulder and calling out my name. As I turned my head to the sound of the voice, I saw my tennis coach, Tawio, trying to wake me from sleep.

> *Stefan, hope you are okay?*

> *Yes, I am fine.*

> *How far nau, wetin happen? Talk to me, because this your sleep nor be ordinary.*

With a deep smile, I replied,

> *nor be small tin oh, na condition make crayfish bend. I for take*
> *small coffee before I comort for house.*

We both burst out in laughter. I apologised to the taxi driver and paid him off.

E H A N | 6

Joseph, my father's oldest driver, was my Pidgin English teacher. He and Teddy taught me all I knew about the language. Growing up in Nigeria, I was eager to learn Pidgin English because my father deliberately never spoke it to us. This also applied to his native Benin language, which took a back seat in our home.

However, I never really felt the impact until my grandmother, whom we called Iye, came to live with us at our Ikpoba Hill home in Benin City, southern Nigeria. My father had spent most of his childhood in her care, and she raised him with all the love in the world, irrespective of how preoccupied she was with her role as one of the founders of a local Juju ritual group. As Iye grew older and weaker, my father felt it was his turn to take care of her. After much persuasion, he finally convinced her to leave her village house and spend her last years in our modern home.

I remember early mornings watching my grandmother perform her daily ritual. She practised it only for constructive purposes.

Each time I watched her shuffle one foot in front of the other, her back bent almost double until her head nearly touched the top of her walking stick. I couldn't imagine my father's descriptions of his mother, who was once one of the most stunning women in the village.

My inability to speak Benin as a child made it almost impossible to communicate with my grandmother, who only spoke and heard the language. This made it hard for me to bond with her. I had many questions but couldn't express myself because of the language barrier, and I couldn't use any of my siblings as an interpreter because none of them spoke the Benin language.

Unlike other Benin families in our hometown, my father spoke only English to us. Guests in our home adjusted to the fact that we were an English-speaking household with varying degrees of success.

Our house-helps were also encouraged to speak English, but Joseph ignored this. Many house-helps arrived from their remote villages unable to utter a word of the foreign tongue, but as the weeks went by, they began to string together complete sentences with less strain on their faces. My parents always communicated in English, despite my father growing up speaking Benin and my mother, Swiss German. The only people my father spoke his local dialect with were his brothers, sisters, and other family members. Whenever I heard him speaking Benin, I knew it was a conversation we were never allowed to interrupt.

Among the many rules that made up the foundation of our household, one of the biggest offences we could commit was speaking Pidgin English. My father was always on alert for the slightest mumble of a word in Pidgin and was ready to discipline us, though I wondered why.
Punishment for me varied. Some days, I knelt outside our house, arms elevated with pitifully apologetic looks. As I grew, I discovered how deeply this history with my language affected how I thought. From an early age, I was conditioned to look down on my father's tongue and to deem it "irrelevant," and to laugh in mockery when I heard people speak "Pidgin or Benin." It was ingrained in me to view one's ability to speak English and speak it impeccably as synonymous with high intellect.

Anyone today would wonder why there was so much disdain for one of Africa's most widely spoken languages. This I blame on the ignorance of my parents' generation.

It may surprise you that Nigerian Pidgin is an English-based Creole language spoken as a lingua franca by approximately 213 million people across Nigeria. The language is commonly referred to as "Pidgin." Broken English (pronounced "Brokin") is not necessarily Pidgin. Broken English refers to poor use of the English language (either spoken or written), the type that the individual struggles to speak fluently and correctly with grammatical errors. Broken has no structure and can exist in any language.

On the other hand, Pidgin is distinguished from other Creole languages since most people who speak it are not native speakers, although many learned it at an early age. Different speakers can say it as a pidgin, a creole, or a decreolised acrolect, and they may switch between these forms depending on the social setting. Variations of Pidgin are also spoken across West and Central Africa in countries such as Equatorial Guinea, Ghana, and Cameroon. Despite its common use throughout these countries, Pidgin English has no official status.

The origins of Nigerian Pidgin English lie historically in trade contact between the British, Portuguese, and local people in the 15th century. It is part of a continuum of English Pidgins and Creoles spoken in other West African countries such as Cameroon, Sierra Leone, and Ghana. In recent years, Nigerian Pidgin English development has been particularly evident in the big cities and ports in the south of Nigeria, where it is used among people belonging to different ethnic groups. The use of this Creole language is strictly linked to the urbanisation process.

Nigerian Pidgin, along with the various Pidgin and Creole languages of West Africa, shares similarities with the various English-based Creoles found in the Caribbean. It is especially obvious in Jamaican Creole (also known as Jamaican Patois or simply Patois) and the other Creole languages of the West Indies.

Linguists posit that this is because most enslaved people taken to the New World were of West African descent. The pronunciation and accents often differ greatly, mainly due to the extremely heterogeneous mix of African languages present in the West Indies, but if written on paper or spoken slowly, the creole languages of the Caribbean are, for the most part, mutually intelligible with the creole languages of West Africa.
The presence of repetitive phrases in Caribbean Creole, such as "su-su" (gossip) and "pyaa-pyaa" (sickly), mirror the presence of such words in West African languages like "bam-bam", which means "complete" in the Yoruba language.

Repetitive phrases are also present in Nigerian Pidgin, such as "koro-koro", meaning "clear vision", "yama-yama", meaning "disgusting", and "doti-doti", meaning "garbage". Furthermore, the use of West African origin words in Jamaican Patois like "Unu" and Bajan dialect "wunna" or "una" - West African Pidgin (meaning "you people", a word that comes from the Igbo word "unu" or "wunna", also meaning "you people") displays exciting similarities between the English pidgins and creoles of West Africa and those of the West Indies, as does the presence of words and phrases that are identical in languages on both sides of the Atlantic, such as "Me go tell dem" (I'm going to tell them) and "make we" (let us).

The word "deh" or "dey" is found in both Caribbean Creole and Nigerian Pidgin English and is used in place of the English word "is" or "are". The phrase "We dey foh London" would be understood by both a speaker of Creole and a speaker of Nigerian Pidgin to mean "We are in London" (although the Jamaican is more likely to say "Wi de a London"). Other similarities, such as "pikin" (Nigerian Pidgin for "child") and "pikney" (used in islands like St. Vincent, Antigua, and St. Kitts, akin to the standard-English pejorative/epithet pickaninny) and "chook" (Nigerian Pidgin for "poke" or "stab") which corresponds with the Bajan Creole word "juk", and also corresponds to "chook" used in other West Indian islands.

Being derived partly from the present-day Edo/Delta area of Nigeria, there are still some leftover words from the Portuguese language in Pidgin English (Portuguese ships traded slaves from the Bight of Benin). For example, "you sabi do am?" means "do you know how to do it?". "Sabi" means "to know" or "to know how to", just as "to know" is "saber" in Portuguese. (According to the monogenetic theory of pidgins, 'sabir' was a basic word in Mediterranean Lingua Franca, brought to West Africa through Portuguese Pidgin (an English cognate is savvy). Also, "pikin" or "pickaninny" comes from the Portuguese words "pequeno" and "pequenino", which mean "small".

Like the Caribbean Creole situation, Nigerian Pidgin is mostly used in informal conversations. However, Nigerian Pidgin has no status as an official language. Nigerian Standard English is used in politics, the internet, and some television programs.

The most important difference from other types of English is the limited repertoire of consonants, 6 vowels, and 3 diphthongs used. This produces many homophones, like thin, thing, and tin, all pronounced like /tin/. This circumstance gives high importance to the context, tone, body language, and any other ways of communication for distinguishing homophones.

In the past, Nigerian Pidgin English was linked to non-educated people and perceived by the educated ones with a negative attitude. Nowadays, Pidgin English is more widespread, even among educated people and is perceived as more Nigerian than English. Indeed, using Pidgin is increasingly popular among young people, writers, and musicians.
The fact that it is not attached to any ethnic group makes it a good candidate as an official lingua franca in Nigeria. The language can also function, in some contexts, as an act of identity when speakers need to stress their 'Nigerianness', as opposed to their ethnic group identity. In other words, Nigerian Pidgin English can express a sense of belonging to Nigeria, which English, the language of the ex-colonial power, cannot. This is very similar to other multiethnic postcolonial situations.

If I were to compare the linguistic situation of the Mauritius Islands, where English and French are the official languages but coexist with other powerful community languages like Chinese, Hindi, Urdu, etc., I would have to acknowledge the unique role of Mauritian French Creole. Despite lacking official status, this language is the only one that can express a neutral Mauritian identity.

No official status has been granted to Pidgin English in Nigeria. However, some Nigerians have suggested it would be a good candidate for national language status since it retains solidarity and neutrality.

But who go do am? Who will grant this unifying lingua franca official status and hand the language its flowers? If e dey for my power, I for don break the mould. Nor be my fault at all. Na condition wey make crayfish bend. If na me dey for that high position as Senate President, I no go just give my dear country solar-powered electricity and water, I for don make Pidgin English the official and national language for Nigeria.

Despite these challenges, Pidgin English is gradually gaining more recognition and acceptance. The entertainment industry in Nigeria is a significant promoter of the language. Musicians such as Fela Kuti, Femi Kuti, Wizkid, and Burna Boy perform in Pidgin, while Nollywood, the Nigerian film industry, is incorporating pidgin dialogue into their movies. This increased exposure has helped the language gain global recognition and acceptance.

The British Broadcasting Corporation (BBC) even has a Pidgin version, and radio stations like WAZOBIA (a term that means "come" in three major Nigerian languages) now broadcast in Pidgin across Nigeria. Additionally, some parts of the Bible have been translated into Pidgin, which further cements its importance in Nigerian culture.

The growing popularity of Pidgin English has turned it into a unifying force for Nigerians at home and in the diaspora. It serves as a symbol of national identity, connecting people of different ethnic backgrounds and fostering a sense of belonging.

But the question remains: when will it dawn on the Nigerian government to grant Pidgin English an official status? In the next twenty, thirty, or forty years? Or now, when all cultural and social factors are, in fact, encouraging it in a nation of over 500 ethnicities? If no be condition wey make crayfish bend, I for don do am since, as our government people no wan gree reason for their citizens. But while all is said and done, this may only likely end as a thought.
"Na condition wey make crayfish bend" is an adage you've seen me use frequently. It is a common saying in Nigeria, used when someone needs to break the law or do something immoral or illegal due to the circumstances at the time. This adage also describes and categorises Nigeria's social hierarchy by age and income. It is a known fact in Nigeria that older people should be treated with the highest respect. A child, whether 5 or 45 years old, would never speak back to their parents or make bodily movements that indicate disrespect when talking with them. A Nigerian child learns from infancy that acting disrespectfully to an older person will result in harsh punishments (such as beatings).

Maids, nannies, security guards, and drivers are employed in many Nigerian homes with over-pampered children. The above criterion does not apply since these people are from a lower socioeconomic class. As a result, the children of their employers, though younger, would speak disrespectfully without fear of repercussions. Because of their socioeconomic status, these people are left with no choice but to cope with disrespect from their employer's children by remarking, "Na condition wey make crawfish bend."

The proverb's metaphor comes from the concept that a crayfish's body should be straight rather than curled. The crayfish's curved nature is thought to represent a less developed version of its initial straight shape. According to this adage, the crayfish's body is twisted because of factors surrounding it, not because the crayfish did anything to earn the deformity.

This proverb carries a lot of weight! Members of less valued social systems, such as nannies, might use this metaphorical claim to respond to their mistreatment. These individuals may not be able to change their circumstances, but this proverb recognises it isn't entirely their fault, and they can use it to emphasise their pains to their superiors in the hopes of being recognised. The Pidgin English metaphor reminds us that circumstances can significantly shape an individual's life. It also allows those in disadvantaged positions to express their experiences and seek understanding.

I H I N R Ọ N | 7

Over the years, I have become obsessed with and worried about the geopolitical space called Nigeria. I believe Nigeria is "Sorgenkind," a German word for "problem child." And just to be clear, I'm not the only one who has this opinion; almost every other Nigerian and non-Nigerian I have met throughout the years, from my parents, siblings, friends, workplace discussions to debates with former classmates and chats with strangers on a remote bus in Peru, have all shared the same view about Nigeria and how behind she is when compared to other developing nations across the world. Most of these discussions were about interventions on fundamental issues affecting the country while trying to connect her to the fast-changing world.

These discussions have continued in the 2 to 3 chat groups I have been a member of. Since the boom of WhatsApp and mobile instant messaging, the creation of groups on social media has grown widely. With Facebook, classmates from my secondary school 32 years ago suddenly remembered I existed and wanted to catch up. When Facebook became 'uncool,' these people migrated to Blackberry Messenger and later moved on to X (formerly Twitter) and now WhatsApp.

My secondary school alumni WhatsApp group, for instance, has over 155 participants from around the world. We also have another chat group with around 50 participants. The latter group is strictly for the United Kingdom.

Messages come in both chat groups constantly, and everybody is trying to figure out who is who—match the phone numbers to the profile pictures—or follow up on active topics and discussions. Then there's the tiny issue of topics discussed, projects, and decision-making. Many of the topics discussed in the group revolve around Nigeria, corrupt government, secondary school, fuel rise, and Nigerian political parties, to name a few!

I can remember a particular day while I was on my lunch break. In just less than 30 minutes, there were over 1700 messages in the group. I was confused; by seven p.m. that same day, my phone had exploded with photos. It was literally like my phone was manned around the clock by different time zones than the other participants.

And the thing was, I could not even complain. If you have been in a chat group comprising Nigerians, then you would know how frustrating it can be to make decisions or complain. From little things like planning the refurbishment of the pupils' desks and chairs to trying to ignite similar project ideas for my old school, my group almost made me want to bang my head against a wall. But the group is not dull. At least the administrators are remarkable, and the members are intriguing.

In fact, I have experienced many fabulous moments with these great classmates, for which I am thankful. My favourite was when our 30th reunion rolled around. I wasn't sure what to expect from the turnout. We were coming from various walks of life, and before the event, most of us only stayed in touch through social media.
Just as every ship needs a skipper, our class was led by a group of fabulous leaders baptised as the' organisation committee'. It comprised ten members who organised the fantastic reunion event at the Clarendon Hotel in Blackheath.

Blackheath, a place that has long been an important meeting point and focus for historical events, was about to give birth to our thirtieth school reunion. This historic venue has been the scene for many social uprisings and battles. For example, Wat Tyler's Peasants Revolt of 1881 was assembled here on the heath, same for the Jack Cade's Rebellion of 1450. Our get-together, however, was not a revolution but rather a festival gathering with a floristic agenda in this old hotel, 6,710 kilometres from our beloved alma mater in Benin City.

Our reunion was blessed with various activities, such as presentations, school quizzes, singing prayers, and old-school songs. One of my highlights was the food, dancing to music hits from the early 90s, and the presence of our then-vice principal, who also delivered a heartfelt speech.

Few things grab us by the collar and humble us as much as our school reunions. They come back every 5 years to haunt us like ghosts from the past. And maybe that's just what's so humbling about them. If there are any lessons I learnt from this reunion in Blackheath, they would be;

First things first, it's all about the people. Moments before our classmates arrived, my anxiety kicked in, and I began overthinking. "Should I run and get a truck stacked with Nigerian meals like pounded yam and Egusi soup? Should we have celebrated in the hotel's wonderful garden? Should we schedule a parallel Zoom session for other class members who are far away? Etc."

Eventually, I discovered I had nothing to worry about because, honestly, no one cared about the bells and whistles. Everyone was so happy to see each other. Though I must confess, name tags would have filled in the blanks of my slipping memory and protected me from awkward moments at the event. While I recognised most classmates personally and from social media, name tags would have been a big help to me, especially with spouses.

Each dining table in the hall was decorated with personalised cards for every seat. However, only a few classmates had recognisable names or portrait pictures on their social media profiles. So, I found myself texting classmates I was familiar with under the table to help me with the names of the others I desperately tried to identify.

Another thing I learnt from this reunion was that it's all love. The thought of a reunion can bring mixed emotions. While some were excited, I tried to remember that the adolescent years were tough for everyone. Our youthful past is exposed once again, laid bare like an open wound, and brutally juxtaposed with our current reality. I was happy to experience that time heals many wounds, and that we held through all this time. We laughed together about high school events (inter-house sports moments, auditorium fails, fine art and metalwork classes, the launch at our famous and beloved kiosk, and memorable teachers).

I also found out that most of my classmates loved horizontal photos. As someone who prefers portrait mode shots, I was perplexed by how many preferred snapping pictures in landscape mode. Well, there was nothing like smartphones during our secondary school days, so that's why I never noticed that.

Finally, I was reminded that life is short. Our MC (Master of Ceremonies) mentioned and honoured a handful of our classmates who had sadly passed away over the years. It was a gentle reminder to hug everyone extra tight when we parted ways.

Secondary school had many cliques and ethnic divides, but the best part of the reunion was seeing how we all came together in the end. It truly felt like family. There were no labels. Nobody seemed to care who my friends were back in the day. We rallied around each other. We celebrated and danced. We discussed future hopes and dreams and even planned the next reunion trip to Cape Town, South Africa. It was a great experience!

In the words of Dr Edward L. Kramer, "No matter who you are or where you may be, you can do something to change the world for the better." That's why I value my alum group and their initiatives.

I remember there was a topic in the chat group about ancestry, and during that period, I learned about a website, MyHeritage.com.

As funny as it may sound, this website revealed that 42.9% of my DNA or ethnicity distribution was mapped to Nigeria. I'm no genealogist, but I had some issues with this proposition.

First, there's no such thing as "Nigerian" ancestry per se, as Nigeria is not an ethnicity. Nigeria has only been an independent nation for 63 years. Like many other African nations that don't reflect the boundaries of ethnicity, the country was formed when

Europeans grouped several major ethnic groups and dozens of minority groups, each with its language, customs, and culture.

Natural migrations and the disruption of the Transatlantic Slave Trade have also caused a certain amount of flux among these groups, so people in one place at a given time may be in a different place 200 years later. Also, Nigeria's Igbo population has had a tradition of taking in people from other ethnicities, so they have dramatically different genetic variations. A reputable DNA test should have given me more precise results based on ethnicity, e.g., 7% Benin, 2% Bantu, etc.

Moreover, the name 'Nigeria' is a product of Lord Lugard's wife, Flora Shaw. Hence, this so-called name is not culturally connected to the people and should not be used to identify anyone's DNA. Let's not forget that Lord Lugard oversaw the forced amalgamation of the region's diverse inhabitants in 1914. I believe he is responsible for many of Nigeria's long-standing issues, including consistently rigged population censuses, fraudulent allocations of seats in the old federation, and the problematic foundations of the country's military and police. Nevertheless, as adults, we must come to terms with the mistakes made before our existence and accept the flawed decisions of our ancestors. It is now our responsibility to take charge and restore our pride.

Surprisingly, wisdom can often be found in the weirdest quotes and sayings and even in the ones we consider "unlearned." Allow me to reference a discussion I had with a friend a while ago to buttress this point. Osarumwense told me of a deep conversation he had with an okada rider (a local commercial bike rider) in the streets of Benin City. What interested me the most in the whole ordeal Osarumwense had with this Okada rider was the proverb he learned from him. In the okada man's words, which he communicated in pidgin, he said, "This world na standing fan. If e blow you small. E go leave you go blow another person." Osarumwense responded in a rather objectionable tone, "For Nigeria, our fan nor dey rotate. The rotation button don spoil, na him make am say, na de same criminals dey office since independence." Osarumwense's friend, who was already soaked in the discussion, quickly chipped in, "And instead of fixing the rotation button, everybody is struggling to stand in front of the fan."

This dialogue encapsulates Nigeria's current tragic situation. After reflecting on it for a while, I came to realise that while the okada rider spoke to the ideal he felt was appropriate; it is difficult to fault the argument raised by Osarumwense that many Nigerians are more concerned with positioning themselves and their families in a spot in front of the standing fan to benefit from the country's resources rather than finding solutions to its problems. This mindset explains why Nigeria is a country besieged today, from the economy to governance and national security. Rather than seeking solutions, everyone is pointing fingers or manoeuvring themselves for a share of the "national cake" at virtually all levels of public engagement.

To better understand Nigeria's predicament, consider these sobering facts: In April 1980, during the Second Republic, a barrel of oil sold for $37.24, and Nigeria pumped 2.2 million barrels daily. At that time, the country's population was around 73.44

million. Today, oil is around $69, and Nigeria pumps around 1.47 million barrels daily. According to the latest United Nations data, Nigeria's population has nearly tripled to 220,810,966. While our population has skyrocketed, our earnings have stagnated as we still depend on oil to fuel our economy. Moreover, we (or, best I say, the government) have mismanaged this valuable resource.

In 2020, the Nigerian National Petroleum Corporation (NNPC) wrote to the Accountant General of the Federation about the financial implications of the subsidy regime that the nation has struggled to let go of. Meanwhile, Shell was increasing dividends for its shareholders for the second time within 6 months. First-quarter earnings surpassed forecasts by an impressive $100 million, rising from $3.1 billion to $3.2 billion. The contrast between Shell and NNPC was striking. The real challenge, however, lies in the implications of the NNPC letter. Based on 2020 statistics regarding the Federation Account Allocation Committee (FAAC) receipts as a percentage share of total revenue, over thirty of the 36 states would face severe difficulties if there were no oil money to distribute in Abuja at the end of each month. In fact, for 9 states, 90% or more of their total earnings come from FAAC allocations.

Sadly, we can't even factor agriculture into this issue, as it has slowed down significantly in the country, especially in the past 3 years, primarily due to criminal activities by bandits, kidnappers, and insurgents.

Yet, numerous elite commentators, both academic and political, have painted a picture of the Nigerian smallholder farmer as "illiterate, backward, and supine." Having lived among them and indirectly shared their cultural life and struggles, I have grown to respect these tenacious producers who have carried the weight of Nigeria on their shoulders in terms of confrontation and resistance against the colonising British, as well as ensuring food security for fellow Nigerians, despite devastating odds like insecurity and insurgency plaguing the agricultural sector.

As I continue, I have chosen to avoid debates surrounding the use of terms like "peasants," "peasantry," and "serf," as it is not my intention to focus on such matters. I will refrain from using these terms.

Nonetheless, mediaeval Europe was built on the unpaid labour of serfs (semi-slaves), who were given a small piece of land in exchange for working without pay on the estates of the church and feudal nobility for several days a week. This arrangement also included manorial duties, which obligated serfs to perform specific tasks for their lords' benefit. Around 1000 BC in England, it is estimated that as much as 70% of the population was classified as serfs. The origins of capitalism can be traced back to the struggles of this oppressed peasant class to free themselves from bondage.

"Stadtluft macht frei nach Jahr und Tag," as the German proverb goes, "town air makes you free after a year and a day." Its origins can be traced back to a Middle Ages customary law that said any fugitive serfs who stayed in a town for a year and a day were no longer subject to their previous lords' claims and therefore became free. This habit, however, did not fall from the heavens or result from a gentleman's agreement between the kings and their slaves. It was the culmination of years of fierce class conflict.

Given the strong militancy demonstrated by the peasants and other marginalised classes in Nigeria against the intrusion of the British into our history over decades, I continue to wonder why there is such sepulchral silence amongst the oppressed classes in the country today. Nigeria remains a nation of peasants, hence still containing attributes of feudalism and capitalism.

From the start of the British criminal expedition in Nigeria, the working class began to emerge when the colonial authority saw the necessity of building a peripheral capitalist system in the nation for its exploitative reasons. Upon their arrival, the peasants who met the invaders simply passed the relay baton to the working class, whose contacts with the capital had prepared it to take on the mission. The workers of Nigeria took on the confrontation with the colonisers in a very vigorous way, often losing limbs and lives to a very ruthless and criminally intentioned enemy.
Let's take a moment to consider the feudal system. Many of today's old and new movies are based on monarchy. Ordinary people's lives are significantly less commonly shown in films. Monarchs, on the other hand, had ultimate control over their subjects, and in Europe, they were governed by a feudal system in which the land and the aristocracy enslaved serfs. They were no better than enslaved people in any way. The film "Robin Hood" is a famous example of what I am trying to illustrate.

Walt Disney has spent almost a century building stories around the benefits of the nobility system. A person anywhere could talk about the despicable nature of slavery and at the same time enjoy a Disney movie about princesses, princes, or even Tarzan, the latter being the king of the African jungle.

How would your perception of a Disney movie change if the story made it clear that Cinderella owned slaves or that Tarzan's parents enslaved people?

If you've ever been on a tour of a palace in France, such as Versailles, Château de Rambouillet, or Château de Maisons, you may have seen that the living conditions of the serfs around the palaces were not mentioned by historians. Even the labourers' working conditions were rarely, if ever, highlighted. You will conclude that this historical explanation of feudalism depends upon an oversupply of labour.

As a society, we rarely associate slavery with royalty or feudal systems. However, it's crucial that we do. Why? Because understanding slavery and serfdom is essential for comprehending the foundations and development of capitalism.

It's important to consider that opposing slavery conditions doesn't mean one should disregard other aspects of corporate practices. For example, while Apple supports the Black Lives Matter movement and advocates for racial justice, being unconcerned about their outsourcing of manufacturing to China could be an oversimplification of the issue.

In a socialist state, capitalism and feudalism do not exist. For socialism to be built, all means of production, such as land, forests, oil, and electricity, must be controlled and owned collectively by the working class, including former peasants and serfs.

Poverty and hunger cannot be eradicated in society without "persuading" those who sow these dilemmas amongst the majority of the people to desist from such heinous activities. It would surely take strong revolutionary politics to achieve this persuasion.

Unlike Russia, which transitioned from serfdom to communism, we Nigerians should create and implement our own socialist objectives, structure, and a new and revamped political movement to guide us to the Promised Land. This new political party should be earmarked for the strengthening and general support of the people's initiatives that foster the basic characteristics of socialism.
According to the World Bank, almost a quarter of Nigeria's workforce was unemployed in 2018, with an additional 20% underemployed. This alarming situation demands urgent attention to tackle the systemic issues hindering Nigeria's progress.

Whichever direction you look, the prognosis for Nigeria has been worrisome. At a certain point, according to the United Nations High Commissioner for Refugees (UNCHR), there were around 2.1 million displaced Nigerians and over 304,562 refugees in 2020 alone. Furthermore, Nigeria is not only known for having the largest population of out-of-school children in the world today but the federal Ministry of Education, an institution responsible for creating and implementing better education policies, has even openly reported its failure by stating that millions of children are dropping out of school annually. What a shame!

From the foregoing, it is clear that the button on the standing fan had long ceased to function, resulting in ventilation reaching only a select few. The challenge, however, is that the blades are also weakening, with the possibility that the fan could eventually stop working altogether. When some of us talk about restructuring Nigeria, it is not about dividing the country for ethnic entrepreneurs, but rather about making the system work for all citizens.

Nigeria has not been functioning effectively, and there is no need to live in denial or pretend that all is well or may improve in the future when all indicators suggest otherwise. A shift in mentality is required; we must focus on providing solutions to our existing and emerging challenges rather than merely seeking a small share of the available resources.

Nigeria could still work because we have the potential. Sub-regions like the Middle Belt, which has suffered immense subjugation, oppression, and repression for nearly a century now, could still flourish. Their expertise in agriculture could make the country the biggest exporter of food to the rest of the world.

The Middle Belt could be reformed to focus on solid mineral development, tourism, and food production and exports. This region has the potential to become a food hub in

West Africa. Mega-mining and food corporations, as well as tourism development, could arise. It may even host some of the most beautiful places to live in Nigeria in the future. Mind you, this is just one of many sub-regions in Nigeria that has so much untapped potential.

So, I still believe Nigeria's future is bright, but it is crucial that we all work collectively to address these underlying problems preventing our greatness, paving the way for a brighter future for all Nigerians.

E H Ẹ N R Ẹ N | 8

The terms "ethnicity", "tribe", and "race" often get mixed up in conversations, but they mean different things. While scientists have found no genetic basis for these classifications, they continue to influence how people live and interact. Both race and tribe remain social categories that people use to separate different groups, affecting relationships and social structures across communities.

Coming from a multi-racial and multi-cultural family, I understand how these categories affect people deeply. They influence how we look, who we feel connected to, and how others treat us. For those of us with mixed racial backgrounds, these identities become particularly significant, shaping our daily experiences and personal relationships in unique ways.

I have always seen people from multicultural backgrounds as special gifts to humanity, showing how different cultures unite beautifully. Through our existence, we demonstrate that people from different backgrounds can live together peacefully. Our presence challenges old prejudices and proves that cultural boundaries can dissolve into something more meaningful and enriching. However, society often fails to see this beauty. Instead, many of us find ourselves struggling to prove we belong, constantly explaining our identity to gain acceptance in places that should naturally welcome us.

I addressed these challenges in my first book, "Caught In-Between," using the African philosophy of "Ubuntu" - which teaches us about human kindness and connection. The book aimed to show how we can build societies based on fairness and mutual respect. Through various personal accounts and research, it explored the complexities of living between multiple cultural identities while maintaining authenticity in each space.

The response to the book revealed something unexpected—many people shared similar experiences of being caught between different cultural identities. This led to the creation of the "Caught In-Between" community, where people found comfort in sharing their stories. The community became a safe space for discussing the unique challenges and joys of having multiple cultural identities in today's world.

This community has grown to include voices from different parts of the world, each bringing unique perspectives on identity and belonging. Now, while protecting their privacy, I want to share some of these stories to show how our experiences connect us, regardless of our ethnic or racial backgrounds. Through these shared experiences, we find strength in our diversity and hope for a future where identity becomes a bridge rather than a barrier.

These stories reveal a universal truth: that human connection transcends the artificial boundaries we create. They show us that our differences, rather than dividing us, can enrich our understanding of what it means to be human in a world that is so small.

A   d   u   n

The first person whose experience I'm about to narrate is someone who, like me, is of two different cultures. His story is very similar to mine because we both know what it means to live between two worlds—him between Nigeria and Switzerland, straddling different cultures and identities.

You know those questions people ask that seem innocent but are actually insulting? Like "Where are you really from?" "Are you half-caste?" "Do people back home see you as different?" He got them all the time, just like I did. Behind those questions was always that same message we both knew too well: "You don't belong here."

Whether in Nigeria or Switzerland, he felt like an outsider. I know that feeling—spending years trying to find your place and constantly feeling like a stranger even in places you call home. The faces and voices might be different, but the message never changes.

We noticed the same thing - how people with just one background would try to ignore the part of us that matched them. It's like they're saying, "Don't try to claim you're one of us when you're not fully like us."

Both of us have lived in different places and seen discrimination, racism, and tribalism up close. As multicultural people, every day, we fight this battle of not belonging, both in our heads and in how we deal with others.

Like me, he found his way to handle it - by standing firm in who he is. When people tried to make him feel like an outsider, he would boldly claim both sides of his heritage.

It takes guts to do that, to demand that people accept you as you are. Because this is who we are—it's not something anyone can change or has the right to question. His story shows how strong multicultural people have to be in a world that constantly judges us.

A l e x s e i

This experience is from someone whose story really touched me—a half-Russian, half-Nigerian man. His story started in Russia, where his father was studying medicine and fell in love with his Russian mother during those cold winters.

Things changed quickly in the early 70s when his mother got pregnant. His father had to drop out of medical school and return to Nigeria, not really by choice.

When his mother married his father, the Russian government took away her citizenship. But she never lost her Russian spirit. She taught her son the Russian language - something he's grateful for to this day.

He grew up speaking Russian and English and wanted to learn his father's tongue, the Igbo language, but his father never cared to teach him. Nigeria has over 250 languages, and English isn't even one of them originally.
His father never taught him Igbo, which affected their relationship because he felt closer to his mother and distant from his father. This reminded me of my father, who refused to teach me his language. But while he was worried about how society would view us speaking Pidgin or Benin, his father's reason was different - he felt the village elders wouldn't accept his son because he didn't look typically Igbo.

His father's love for Igbo culture, which started as something good, became too much. It caused problems, especially when his father would question his choice of friends based on their tribe. They fought about everything—race, culture, and religion. Even though they were both Christians, they still found things to argue about, from football teams to schools. It was like my own fights with my father, but worse.

The whole thing came to a head when he brought home his Serbian girlfriend. His father insisted on an Igbo wife, typical Nigerian father behaviour, if you ask me.

But he had the perfect counter. He asked his father point-blank why he married a Russian woman (his mother) then. The silence that followed was heavy. His mother was crying, his father couldn't speak, and that was the last time he saw his father.

But don't worry, the story has a happy ending. He married that Serbian woman and their son speaks three languages. Now, their son is with an African woman, and they couldn't be happier. It just shows how beautiful it is when different cultures come together.

L a o i s e

This next experience is about a woman born to a Chinese mother and an Irish father. Growing up in Dublin, many people often couldn't figure out where she was from. Like me, being of 2 different cultures shaped every part of who she became.

From a young age, she was very interested in her mother's Chinese background. By age7, she could speak Mandarin and Irish fluently—imagine that! Her fascination with her cultural background was so profound that while her classmates focused on local Irish landmarks for school projects, she was intrigued by the Great Wall of China. No wonder she later became a history teacher; her love for culture and history was a passion she wanted to share, and teaching offered her the best medium to do so.

Her parents did a great job of keeping her connected to both sides. They celebrated everything—from Chinese New Year to St. Patrick's Day. But things changed when she was 9. She had to fill out a form for the swimming club, and there was no way to show she was Chinese and Irish. That's when she knew she couldn't be reduced to one label. Her heritage was not a limitation, but an asset.

She cherished her origins and the unique perspectives they brought to her life, forming a strong connection with her cultural roots. As she shared with our community, she had to face many incidents of racism. She said her mixed identity made people give different wrong assumptions about her and what she may or may not know.
For instance, her Asian appearance made people assume she could direct them to the nearest sushi restaurant, regardless of where she was.

Her cultural expertise was doubted in her Irish history classes, with some students refusing to accept her knowledge on the subject. She challenged these assumptions, once even turning a disrespectful incident into an intensive teaching moment and a lesson in humility for a racially insensitive student.

People had many wrong ideas about her - what she liked, how much money her family had, the whole package. Sometimes, they'd treat her like she was strange, and other times like she was weird. But she learned to ignore all that nonsense, just like I had to.

These days, she doesn't see herself as half of anything. She's fully Chinese AND fully Irish - no need to choose.

I z e g b e

Raised in a Benin and Igbo home, the woman I'm about to share her experience, felt closer to her father's Benin side. But this didn't make life easy, especially with all the hostility between both tribes.

In her own words: "Growing up, Benin was a big part of who I was, but love had other plans when I met Kenneth, an Igbo man. My papa no gree at all. Being both Benin and Igbo was hard enough - it felt like I was standing in the middle of an old fight between my parents' people. But you see, love doesn't care about tribe.

My father was deeply into tribalism because of what he saw during the Nigeria-Biafra civil war. But me? I saw Kenneth for who he was—just a sweet man who would even send Hallmark cards to our house."

"Everything changed when I attended Federal Government Girls College (FGGC) in Benin. That's where I really saw Nigeria - making friends with Hausas, Yorubas, everybody. I realised we're all the same people wearing different tribal labels. This helped me when I decided to go to UI (University of Ibadan), even though it was in Yoruba land. My father was not happy with my choice to attend school outside of Benin. 'They are wicked!' he kept saying about Yorubas. But I stood my ground. After all, I had lived with Yoruba girls in FGGC Benin—we shared food, gist, everything. But UI opened my eyes to how deep tribalism runs. The way Yorubas, Igbos, and Benins were carrying the same tribal hatred as my father - it was shocking. But it taught me plenty."

At the time when she told me this story, Nigeria was marking 54 years of independence. She said she was grateful for her time at FGC because it showed her that Nigeria could actually work if we let it. That's what we need to fight this tribalism that won't leave us. "Last I heard, Kenneth don marry Igbo woman and they're expecting. Me sef happy for dem." She said she hopes this tribalism that her father's generation holds onto will end with them. The future is in our hands - young people who can learn new ways of thinking.

Being from 2 tribes showed her that your origin shouldn't box you in. We all must work together to build a Nigeria where love is stronger than our tribal differences.

C h e v y

"When I was born, my parents named me 'Chivy' - it means life. I was still a baby when we had to run away from Pol Pot to France. My yeay (grandmother) always told me this old saying: 'When culture dies, the nation dies. When culture lives, the nation lives.' She would say this again and again, like she was afraid I'd forget.

Before all the killing, Cambodia was powerful - like a giant spreading across Thailand, Vietnam, and Laos. But then Pol Pot came. My yeay said we lost nearly 3 million people. Even now, it hurts to talk about it.

These days, I'm both Cambodian and French, but sometimes, I feel like neither. You know what's funny? I don't even like our traditional foods, like Amok trey, Kuy teav, and Nom Banh Chok, that much. My relatives in Cambodia say I'm different, not really Cambodian anymore. Maybe they're right.

Nobody knows I'm Cambodian when I speak French until they see my face. And when I speak Khmer, my family always points out my French accent. But I don't really care about any of that. I've embraced my nature, and I love my uniqueness.

The stories yeay used to tell me about neak ta (spirits) of the land and water, about our sacred dances - I wish I understood them better. Sometimes, I think about Preah Kit Mealea, our ancient king, watching me struggle between two worlds - not quite at home in France, but drawn to our spiritual world.

In both places, people look through me like I'm a ghost. My dark Khmer skin makes me invisible sometimes. The only place I feel at home is in the French' ghetto' - far from the Cambodia my parents knew.

My parents tried to live like they were still in Cambodia, but in France. It didn't work. They didn't know how things worked here, and it made life hard for me and my brothers and sisters.

The small things hurt, too. Like when I went to the employment office (ANPE), and the man there couldn't believe a Khmer woman could be an architect. To him, I could only be a secretary. He saw my pen, my skirt, and my glasses, but couldn't see me as an architect.

The worst part about being a migrant? No matter how hard you try to fit in, you're always the 'other.' They don't see your rights as a woman; they don't care about any of the 'French values' they are supposed to uphold. It's almost like you're invincible around them. But I am more than what they see. I am Chivy - strong, different, always looking for my place in this world."

E b u n o l u w a

"Growing up in Abeokuta, our compound was always alive with family festivals. We would gather in front of our shrine room every other week, where both saints and Orisha deities watched over us. We'd sit there with our small cups and offerings, enjoying jollof rice and this special spicy black beans and rice recipe — a recipe my grandparents brought back from Cuba. These celebrations really showed me who we were as a people.

But my friends didn't understand me and my family at all. While they were going to the Catholic Church on Sundays, our family was doing something completely different - with our chanting and dancing to the gods. They would laugh at me, saying I was worshipping 'fake' gods and making fun of our white clothes and the language we used during worship.
By the time I was in year 7 in secondary school, things got worse. Nobody wanted me in their circles or activities because my parents were Orisha priests. It was not easy! But even though it pained me, I didn't abandon our ways. Throughout secondary school, I

faced severe bullying and threats, but I focused on my books and came out with one of the best results.

One Saturday, my father called me to our courtyard. As he sat on this old iroko stool, he started telling me about our history and why I shouldn't feel ashamed of our religion or feel forced to become Christian. "Live and let live," he would say about other people's religions.

He took me back to the 18th century, telling me how our great-great-grandfathers worked hard to uplift Orisha religion. He explained how our faith came from West and Central Africa, showing how humans connected with divine ancestors. Even when Islam came in the 9th century, and some African countries started accepting Christianity in the 1500s, Orisha was still the dominant religion in West Africa. It shaped how people lived, traded, and governed.

This made me want to learn more about Orunmila, our god of wisdom and knowledge. The stories say he used to visit Earth as a human priest, teaching people about Ifa. The Ifa text has 256 books called Odu, but only priests can learn them. These books talk about everything in life, and Orunmila helps followers see their future.

My father compared Orunmila to "Wisdom" in the Bible's Book of Proverbs. When I found out many people in my family were Initiates of this practice, I felt so proud. Even in university, some people still had their wrong ideas. When I did well in school, they said it was juju or witchcraft. But I didn't mind them. Instead, I focused on improving my communication skills so I could express myself better and learn different Nigerian languages—Igbo, Hausa, and, of course, Yoruba.

These days, I help initiate people into our tradition. I've collected stories and wisdom from our elders here in Nigeria, and even from those practising Orisha in Brazil and Cuba. I'm keeping these stories for the next generation.

What makes me happier now is how united my family is in our faith. We don't care if outsiders accept us or not—what matters is that we believe in something that truly fulfils us. It's what our people have believed in for generations, and we've put our whole hearts into it."

If there is anything to learn from these stories I've just shared, it's that our personal experiences with discrimination often stem from various factors - religion, skin colour preferences, surnames, and physical traits.

These forms of prejudice, whether favouring fair skin over dark, certain religious beliefs over traditional ones, or specific ethnic features over others, have historical roots. While these biases share similarities with racism, they represent distinct forms of discrimination.

From my observations in Nigeria and across the world, the preference for lighter skin remains a persistent issue as we move towards more multicultural societies. Even after five centuries since the slave trade began, this bias continues to affect communities profoundly. Colourism operates as a form of internal racism within racial groups, where your skin shade can determine how society perceives your social status and beauty. Unfortunately, lighter skin tones often receive preferential treatment.

This form of discrimination isn't new. Before the slave trade, various communities faced similar oppression, including Native Americans thirteen thousand years ago and the Incas five hundred years ago. Yet society still struggles to embrace diversity as a strength rather than a source of division.

While many discussions about multiculturalism focus on class discrimination, and social movements emphasise racial prejudice, few studies examine how class and skin colour work together to create discrimination. These two factors - class and colour - don't compete for relevance; they work together to shape how people experience discrimination. Both social class disadvantages and skin colour preferences influence how society ranks different groups. However, many people find it difficult to identify the exact source of the discrimination they face.

This complexity shows why we need to understand discrimination better. As someone who has experienced these intersecting forms of prejudice, I believe recognising these patterns is the first step toward creating meaningful change in our communities. It's easy to get lost in our personal struggles and daily dramas. However, we must remember that many others carry even heavier burdens. Our actions matter more than our words, and we should show appreciation for people while they are still here with us.

Building a community requires genuine involvement, not treating it like a business venture. I remember some yogis telling me that the real essence of yoga lies in the journey to the mat, not just the practice itself. When I think about how the wisdom from my multi-cultural background has become part of who I am today, I feel both proud and grateful.

For those of us who practise traditional spirituality, we believe our ancestors continue to live through us. And by preserving and practising their teachings, we honour their memory and keep their wisdom alive.

My wish is that we learn to live together in harmony. Ubuntu, a profound philosophy from Southern Africa that teaches the importance of harmonious living, is one of Africa's most valuable contributions to global wisdom. In practice, Ubuntu shows us that the bonds that hold a community together are stronger than any differences we might have. While people will always have disagreements and arguments, Ubuntu teaches us to work towards consensus in community matters. Once we reach this agreement, it represents what's best for everyone, and we must support it.

I believe we should stop judging relationships by how others treat us and embrace the Ubuntu principle that says, 'I am because we are.' This shift in thinking reminds us that our individual existence gains meaning through our connections with others.

To protect the privacy of certain individuals their names and identifying details have been changed.

I H I N R I N | 9

It was a fine Sunday morning. I could feel my phone vibrating, its buzz cutting through my sleep. I guess it was what woke me up. I stretched my hands, still heavy with sleep, and grabbed it from the bedroom stool where it was and pulled the small machine to my face. Lo-and-behold, the alarm I had set last night was staring at my face, and I wondered, "Why would I set an alarm on a Sunday?"

As if a thunderbolt struck my mind, sending a jolt of realisation through me, I instantly recalled telling Teddy yesterday afternoon that he would accompany me on a sightseeing expedition in Lagos today.

"Shit!" It was already six, and my alarm was set for five-thirty with a reminder at six o'clock in the morning, so I had little time to prepare, but I was determined to make the most of it. Despite the rush, I knew this would be worth it. Teddy and I were about to go on an expedition in search of an old Brazilian house in Lagos, a grimy metropolis of 20 million people teeming with history and modernity.

But Teddy was quite grumpy this early morning as he had slept very poorly, tossing and turning all night, as he later told me. He verified it with me by asking if I still wanted to go on the cumbersome trip, his voice heavy with sleep and mild irritation. I replied, "Yes," with a big smile, hoping to see the "Ilojo Bar" building. This monument was originally built as a bar and restaurant in 1855 by Chief Antonio Oladeinde Fernandez, one of the prominent figures in Lagos's architectural history.

You may not have known, but following slave abolition, which was passed on the 25th of March, 1807, there was a wave of liberated Africans returning home that lasted over 5 decades. Armed with architectural knowledge from former slave ports—Brazil, the Caribbean, and even the West Indies—these freed slaves returned home with a specific duty to give back to their communities and optimise their gained knowledge to build historic structures that would, later on, be known as monuments, standing as testaments to their resilience and skill.

In the following years, the steady March of skyscrapers spurred local residents to form a fledgling historic preservation movement, a rarity for an African city like Lagos. This movement made me concerned about Brazilian houses, which were falling apart and on the verge of being destroyed in the future, victims of rapid urbanisation.

Hence, I was more interested in visiting the Ilojo bar. Before I explain the discovery of the Ilojo Bar, I must first share our danfo experience from Oshodi to Tinubu, which would prove to be an adventure in itself.

Our trip started in Oshodi. We needed about 3 different Danfo buses and one Molue bus (the larger, more crowded version) to arrive at our final destination, Tinubu Square. This square was named after a slave trader named Madam Efunroye Tinubu. Some history books paint her as an unapologetic and profit-minded character, though her legacy in Lagos remains controversial.

Lagos is the most commercial state in Nigeria and is home to both lazy and hardworking people. An ordinary citizen in Lagos, just like everyone else, will hustle for the day, not bothering or fretting about tomorrow - living the true 'Lagos no dey carry last' spirit. One general notion, widely believed and widely accepted by all, is that everyone in Lagos now claims to have a "toutish" nature, that street-smart aggression necessary for survival. Nobody wants to be a victim anymore. Even the elite now practise hooliganism on the streets with other drivers, commercial or private, trading insults through wound-down windows of air-conditioned cars.

The journey from Oshodi to Tinubu Square is roughly 17 kilometres and should take about thirty minutes on a good day in Lagos. The problem is, there are no good days in Lagos due to traffic - 'go-slow' as we call it here. In fact, it will take us a 'minimum' of two hours to complete this journey of just 17 kilometres, and remember, I said a minimum. The sun would make sure we remembered every minute of it.

We stood by the roadside in our Lagos-made slippers, the kind everyone wears for comfort in this heat, trying to rant for a Danfo, yelling, *Oshodi, Oshodi,* like seasoned Lagosians.

We heard,

> *Oke, enter with your 100 Naira change; 1000, 500, no enter, cos I no get change o, abeg I no fit fight ooo…*

the conductor chanted, his voice carrying the typical Lagos toutish commanding tone. The journey seemed so short at first, but I never knew I was bracing up for what was going to be the longest journey of my life. Teddy found a seat at the front of the Danfo, lucky him, whilst I had to go in the back, squeezed between other passengers.

> *Abeg Money for front, hold your change, I no get change oh, the conductor reminded everyone.*

I changed position to retrieve my wallet from my back pocket to pay the lousy conductor who kept nagging at everybody. I performed the familiar Lagos dance of trying not to touch anyone while reaching for my pocket.

> *Ogbeni, you sha see say na 200-hundred-naira I give you,*
> *abeg try gimme my change sharp sharp.*

I deepened my voice to make him calm his nerves and respect my personality, which was kinda weird, though, but as I said, nobody wants to be a victim in Lagos. It's either you show them you're tough, or they walk all over you - that's the unwritten rule of the streets.

> *Oga, I don hear, I go give you your change, he replied with a smile that*
> *revealed his teeth, though we both knew getting that change*
> *would be another battle entirely.*

I was looking forward to getting down at our bus stop, already feeling the strain of the cramped space. I noticed that I felt empty, but I couldn't detect why. I was only concerned about getting off the bus as soon as possible. The stern-looking guy beside me kept adjusting himself, shifting towards me, and saying sorry. He had a bag on his lap; his hands were under the bag as if he was hiding something, but I paid no attention - though in Lagos, that's usually the first sign that you should actually pay attention.

> *Oshodi wa o! I shouted as the bus made its way towards our bus*
> *stop, my voice joining the chorus of other passengers signalling*
> *their stops.*

> *Sorry, bros, I want to come down, I excused the rough guy beside*
> *me, already feeling uneasy about his presence.*

As I made my way down the bus, I noticed how he kept looking at me like a lion that had just had his fair share of prey - that satisfied, almost smug look that would soon make terrible sense.

As I turned to continue my walk, I noticed my phone was missing. Then the big picture crept in, hitting me like a punch to the gut; the guy beside me, his bag on his lap and his hands underneath, kept re-adjusting and would say sorry.

> *Shit!*

Classic Lagos pickpocket technique, and I'd fallen for it.

> *You dey find your phone? Teddy asked with a strange look on his face,*
> *that knowing look of someone who'd seen this scene play out before.*

*Yes, O, I replied, tapping my pockets and turning around to see if
it had fallen, though deep down, I knew exactly what had
happened.*

*Na that guy wey dey your side carry am. You no see say he no
dey comfortable? Teddy informed me after a few minutes of joining me to look
around for it.*

Na so dem dey do, awon oloshi (these thieves).

Teddy said sarcastically, even though he was not pleased with the tragic incident and
would have pursued the bus if he could. But boys will always be boys, and in Lagos,
sometimes you just have to laugh to keep from crying.

*You have just experienced what we call commercial bus theft here
in Lagos. With this said, I officially welcome you to Lagos State,
Nigeria, a state of Justice and Pro…gress, he said, laughing weird, like really
weird.*

Or maybe that's how he normally laughs, and I was just being too sentimental because
of my stolen phone. The irony of the state motto wasn't lost on either of us.

*Does this look like a joke to you? I asked in an infuriated tone, my
hands still patting my empty pockets out of habit.*

Luckily, I had 2 phones on me; the stolen one was the phone with my Nigerian number -
a small mercy in this mess.

I eventually told Teddy, "Abeg shift jare, make I pass." As I pushed him playfully out of
my way, I realised that this incident was indeed humorous in some form, just another
page in the endless book of Lagos street wisdom.

We arrived in Tinubu at around eight-thirty a.m., the morning sun now fully awake and
beating down on us, and made our way promptly towards Olufuyi Street, where the
Ilojo Bar had been living since its birth in 1855. Suddenly, to my surprise, merely 20
metres away from my location, I saw an atypical 2-story layout that made me
momentarily forget about my stolen phone. The structure had similarities with a
traditional Yoruba building, with very plain and flat mud walls that seemed whitewashed
but were extended with formal elements like floral decorations and tiled roofs - a perfect
blend of African and Brazilian architectural styles. The building was decorated in an
ornate style, with rounded doorways and windows with pointed tops that seemed to
reach toward the sky. The windows were like Gothic pointed arches. Apart from its great
structural and architectural importance, this building, standing proud despite its age,
reminded me of the tales of our ancestors on slavery plantation fields and the
improvement of their motherland after the abolition of the slave trade.

Walking through one of the many entries, I noticed more profound functional changes. For instance, the layout of the Yoruba House, as I mentioned above, with its sequence of courtyards and its inherent organisation of the family, was often abandoned and replaced with a multi-level design that allowed for more privacy - a revolutionary concept for its time. The introduction of windows, those Gothic-inspired arches I'd noticed earlier, also had a profound effect on daily life, as the new type of indoor living room took on the functions of the courtyard. Subsequent alterations to these buildings reflect the changing family structures in the early 20th century, each modification telling its own story of cultural evolution.

I felt the Ilojo bar was telling a story, speaking of heritage and displaying years of history in every crack and crevice. It was sad to see that the building had not been refurbished or touched in decades. It was currently numbed and dying off among corrupt leaders unwilling to protect its heritage, another victim of Lagos's rush toward modernisation. Standing at the corner of this old art piece, we met an old man leaning against the wall as if he were part of the building's history himself. His name was Area; he carried a cane and wore a loose green sweater with a Masonic symbol chain hanging around his neck. Teddy told him we needed information on the man they called the legendary Victor Olaiya, who had a guitar shop where King Sunny Ade got his guitars. "Bni, bni," the old man exclaimed with a facial expression that suggested he knew who we were talking about.

Victor Olaiya was renowned, so everybody knew and respected him around here. The man contributed more to Nigeria's highlife music than anyone could imagine.

After a few minutes of description, Area was entirely sure of who we were looking for. He asked us to follow him, and we walked through Ilojo with him until we arrived at the defunct old shop where King Sunny Ade got his guitars in the old days. Standing just inside the doorway was a girl wearing rollerblades talking on a cell phone. Beside her was an old man in a leather golf cap smoking a cigar on a backless wooden chair that was about to fall apart, the smoke curling up into the musty air. I said to myself, "This is Lagos!" For a minute or two, I felt I had been teleported back to the 1950s, the past and present colliding in this single moment.

I could tell Area must have been in his late 70s. He was blessed with great and deep knowledge, was well-articulated, and had a good command of the English language. I asked him if any other Brazilian buildings were around, eager to learn more.

He smiled and replied, with that typical Lagos elder's sass,

You no learn history for school? You suppose know all these tins nau.

Teddy and I burst into laughter, and I replied,

we go school but Teacher teach us nonsense.

Area smiled and asked,

Area laughed hard.

As we walked, Area mentioned a couple of building names. There was the "Vaughan-Richards," "Water House," and the "Shitta Bey Mosque," which were built around 1891. To be honest, I only knew of Ilojo Bar as I discovered it whilst undergoing my interior carpentry training back in Switzerland, but I was glad I learnt about the other buildings from Area.

We said our goodbyes to him and squeezed some hard currency in his soft palms to appreciate his services. AsAs we were about to walk away, Teddy whispered, "What a tremendous man he is!". Well, I couldn't agree more.

Teddy and I made our way back to Oshodi, and the evening traffic was now in full swing. On the bus back, I just couldn't stop reflecting on the home of American musician Elvis Presley, which generates an average of 40 million dollars yearly as tourism proceeds—a stark contrast to how we treat our own historical monuments here in Nigeria. The sooner we understand our heritage and history's aesthetic and financial value, the better for us as a nation.

Arriving in Oshodi, exhausted but fulfilled, Teddy and I couldn't help but enter a nearby "mama put", a place where cooked food is sold by a woman at low prices from a handcart or stall. The lady graced us with 2 big portions of pounded yam and Egusi, accompanied by 2 bottles of Star beer, cold enough to make us momentarily forget the day's heat. The rest of the evening was calm, the food and beer working their magic, and I retired to my room for a good night's sleep.

In what seemed like a peaceful sleep, I heard someone calling my name. "Could this be a dream?" I thought subconsciously. I finally opened my eyes only to find Teddy extremely close and tapping my shoulders, trying to wake me up, his face bearing news I didn't want to hear.

He said the radio just broke the news of the demolition of the place we visited yesterday! I am like billions of bilious blue blistering barnacles!! What is wrong with Nigeria? Apparently, the Ilojo Bar was surrounded by street boys whilst the bulldozer was breaking the building apart piece by piece, destroying in hours what had stood for over a century and a half.
At a time when Nigeria suffers from a recession and looks to tourism as a source of revenue, this demolition is perplexing—no, infuriating. Of Nigeria's many monuments, landmarks, and heritage sites, most, like the Kano Walls and Benin Moats, are in a state of worrying disrepair, slowly crumbling under the weight of neglect.

As more national monuments are lost, their stories buried under rubble and progress, we must ask ourselves, what becomes of a society without relics and monuments? What stories will we tell our children when we demolish our history? The Ilojo Bar may have been demolished, but in due time, its tourist value will haunt Lagos and its foolish leaders.

I G B E | 1 0

In December 1975, my mother stepped onto Nigerian soil, carrying me in her womb as she journeyed into what would become her new home. I shall tell more about this experience in the coming chapter, but for now, let me focus on her settlement in the Mid-Western region of Nigeria, housing both Benin and Delta provinces.

Just three months after she arrived, they renamed the Midwestern region to Bendel State. The name change, in fact, was the simple part; what came before that is what I will describe as "the Nigerian Crisis post-civil war." The situation in Nigeria in the 70s could be likened to the Kenyan crisis of 2007—the political tensions and instability were unimaginable.

With the different coups my mother experienced, sometimes I wonder how she managed with 3 children under her care in a strange land where she knew nobody at first. Even the air she breathed was different from what she knew before.

She was strong—that I can admit, because when I look at how things are nowadays, I ask myself: if it were me, would I have survived? I don't think so.

Her first experience of Nigeria was dramatic. She landed here just after General Yakubu Gowon was removed from power and the late Brigadier Murtala Mohammed took over.

This coup made the boundary crisis in Nigeria worse. Communities were fighting bloodily over land. The situation was so serious that Murtala, the new head of state, had to address the nation. He set up a panel to look into the country's boundary crisis, and on December 23, 1975, they brought their report to him.

Murtala was in a hurry to implement everything in that report; after all, he had stepped on big toes when he removed Gowon from power. He knew his time as Head Of State might be short. So, in his rush to create a legacy, he moved the federal capital from Lagos to Abuja and wanted to settle all the boundary problems, but many community leaders across the country did not support his strange and rapid method of resolving the conflict.

Some people will say, "Is he not the head of state? Why can't he just force it?" But you see, in Nigeria, where your tribe matters more than anything else in choosing leaders, even today, such thinking cannot work. Unlike Idi Amin and Thomas Sankara, who were like demi-gods in their countries, the military heads in Nigeria understood their limits to authority, and Murtala did not want anybody to rise against his government.

So what did he do? He created another clever plan by setting up a second panel with Mamman Nasir in charge. This panel was to reassess the boundary crisis, but this time, in collaboration with local community leaders, and then suggest new solutions. Because of their suggestions, my mother experienced the following boundary changes: from Mid-Western Region to Bendel State, and later to Edo State.

When she came to Nigeria in 1975 to settle in Oregbeni, she met the old Mid-Western state. Before she could settle in, it was renamed Bendel State three months later, and its capital remained in Benin City.

Nowadays, if I tell my kids I didn't grow up in the city of Benin, it may be hard for them to comprehend what I'm trying to say after a quick Google search. Oregbeni and Ikpoba Villages were regions completely detached from Benin City when I was growing up. Oregbeni existed as a village long before 1960. It experienced and transitioned through all phases of the boundary adjustment programs, which can be traced back to Nigeria's independence. While I find it displeasing how the Nasir-led panel defrauded Bendel State of its lands and oil wells while making its boundary adjustment suggestions, I'm glad Oregbeni wasn't affected.

Oregbeni transited from the Western Region in 1960 to the Mid-Western Region in 1963, Bendel in 1967, and Edo State in 1991. To me, this town was like an unloved child that has been passed on to various adoptive parents. Oregbeni always remained within the boundaries of any state or region surrounding it, but its surroundings never really changed how it functioned. This town is and remains a self-functioning agglomeration. It had everything it needed to survive. Even the Biafra War posed no threat to its way of functioning.

Growing up, I always identified my location with Oregbeni, not Benin City. I remember my first day in secondary school when my teacher and I got into a small debate over my location. She walked into the class that day with a register. She was staring at it repeatedly and called out to me.

Stefan Asemota!

Present, Ma!

Please, come.

I walked straight to her desk, though I was confused about why I was being singled out of the class.

Where do you live? she asked with a weird look.

I live in Oregbeni, ma.

Then why did you tick the 'out of city' box on your registration file?

Because Oregbeni is out of the city, ma.

How is Oregbeni out of the city? Is it not in Benin City? She questioned me as if she hoped I would reply differently.

No, ma. It is not in Benin City; I do not live in Benin City.

At this point, the whole class was laughing, but I was certain it was not at me but at the drama they were experiencing on their first day of school.

She sighed deeply and said, "Well, my dear Stefan, I know Oregbeni is not as developed as other parts of Benin City, but it is still part of Benin City, okay?"
I looked at her in shock; I guess she could see the shock on my little face. "Don't worry, go back to your seat; I will correct it for you," she said and walked away.

I was still in shock as I walked back. I could not understand the words I just heard my teacher say. Oregbeni, not developed? Did she know how huge this town was? While I would have loved to engage her in a heated debate on the advancements of my village, I did not want my mother to find out that I was debating with my teacher on my first day of school.

At the industrial level, Oregbeni was perhaps the only town in Nigeria with 2 breweries (the Bendel and Guinness breweries). While the former was nothing more than a fraud scheme, the latter still stands as one of the largest breweries in Nigeria. Then, why should anyone call a town with this level of industrialisation "not as developed," like where else in Benin City has this level of development? None!

Even in education, Oregbeni still leads as the home of Western Boys High School, a.k.a. Airewele High School, where the late Dr Samuel Ogbemudia, an old governor of the defunct Bendel State, finished. Airewele was the first privately owned secondary school in Nigeria, founded by Senator Chief Airewele in 1947. Most schools during this pre-colonial era were either owned by missionaries or the government.

Although the school was initially at East Circular in Benin City, it was later moved to Oregbeni because of expansion and was then taken over by the Bendel government in the early 70s because of a government decree that required all private school owners and missionaries to relinquish ownership of their schools to the government.

How, then, can such a town be described as "not developed"? While I may have been offended when my teacher made this remark back in the day, I now understand why she reasoned that way: ignorance and a lack of proper indoctrination of how advanced some unpopular towns in Edo State are.

To be fair, I think Edo State is currently struggling because of the same "ignorance" and lack of "indoctrination." Nothing has changed much over the years, and no one is learning. I mean, we are in the 21st century and still battling to reclaim our lands and oil wells that were unjustly yielded to other states because of their political influence. While Edo State can brag about having one of Nigeria's richest cultural heritages, we have no political relevance in the scheme of things. Why? Our ancestors failed to indoctrinate, and I don't blame them much because they were ignorant.

As I proceed, it's good that you understand that the Benin kingdom is the largest and most recognised monarchy structure in Edo State. While Edo State comprises many tribes like the Benins, Esans, Owans, and Afemais, the word "Edo" is the language of the "Benins," and because the Benins are the largest ethnic group of the state, accounting for over 65% of the population, their language, Edo, is used ceremoniously as the name of the state in present-day Nigeria. Hence, the name "Edo State."
The Benin Kingdom was a monument of human advancement—no exaggeration. What we did with bronze sculptures wasn't mere craftsmanship; it was a historical chronicle, a way to capture political and spiritual moments in metal. With engineering knowledge, this society constructed the Walls of Benin—a mix of ramparts and ditches that equally deserve recognition, like the Great Wall of China.

We didn't get involved in the slave trade either, unlike what most Western sources claim. I personally find their narratives biased and misleading. You can go to Google now and type in "the Great Benin Kingdom and slavery," and what you will find are misleading narratives about our involvement in the slave trade.

I highly doubt that these Western writers ever engaged with the works of the late Chief Dr Jacob U. Egharevba. They seem blissfully unaware of how the name "Edo," representing our language, came about, much less Benin customs and traditions. Their rush to taint all African tribes with the stain of slave trading conveniently deflects the blame and contempt their own history of enslavement has brought upon them.

Did the Benins own slaves? Of course, we did. Slave ownership is as old as the record of human activity itself. But our interaction with slaves was worlds apart from the sadistic dehumanisation that characterised European enslavement. There's not a scrap of historical data that would suggest otherwise. On the contrary, the Benins have a history of elevating their slaves—making them into legends. Oba Ewuare Ogidigan offers a striking example.

Western writers with scant knowledge of Benin culture don't realise that Oba Ewuare, one of the most magnificent rulers to emerge from the Benin lineage, owed his life to a slave named Edo. This slave's name would later be used to identify the geographical territory of the Benins as well as our language.

Here's the story: Prince Ogun found himself in a serious conflict with his brother, Oba Uwaifiokun, which could have easily led to his death. It was Edo, a slave serving Chief Ogiefa Nomuenkpo, who put his life on the line to save him.
This slave understood the danger Prince Ogun was in when he learned of the news that his master had gone to the palace to inform Oba Uwaifiokun (Prince Ogun's younger brother) of his whereabouts after hiding him in the dry well at his compound. This is according to the account of Benin historian Chief Jacob U. Egharevba.

Upon obtaining this information, Edo acted against his master's interest to save Prince Ogun by offering him a ladder and showing him how to escape to avoid being caught by the soldiers already marching into the compound.

But this bold action to go against his master cost him everything. Edo was hanged to death by Chief Ogiefa Nomuenkpo near where the Iya Ero Moat passes today.

However, his story didn't die with him. When Prince Ogun ascended the throne to become Oba Ewuare, he immortalised Edo in a way that etched his name into the annals of time. The city was renamed after this slave, Edo, and so was our language. Today, that slave's name has become the most potent symbol of the Benin people.

This is a simple reflection of how the Benins viewed their slaves—not as commodities to be traded, raped, and brutalised, but as humans worthy of respect and dignity. I challenge these biased Western writers to find a single Western coloniser who would honour a slave to the extent of renaming their land after him. They cannot even think of such a thing! To them, it would be like a taboo.

The truth is that the Benin people always understood the intrinsic value of human life. We have always acknowledged that courage, honour, and integrity were not the sole province of the nobility or the freeborn. These virtues could manifest in any human, even a slave.

It's a shame, then, that this facet of Benin culture, which should have been one of its most celebrated aspects, often remains tucked away in the footnotes of history—eclipsed by the glaring stereotypes and misconceptions perpetuated by those with a vested interest in keeping African stories as one-note tragedies.

Let it be clear: we, the Benin people, even in the throes of slavery, upheld human values that most of the world wouldn't realise until centuries later. As someone fortunate enough to come from a family with close ties with the Benin royal family and being the grandson of the personal translator of Oba Akenzua II, I find it both awe-inspiring and deeply tragic that this understanding of basic human decency was present in my Edo ancestry but got overshadowed by the narratives of those who had none of it.

I remember my visit to the Oba palace years ago, during the famously celebrated Igue festival. An "Igue festival" is an occasion to celebrate the Ugie-Evhoba, an anniversary of the long lineage of Obas, and a way of asking for their blessings on the incumbent Oba and the general populace. It's usually a 7-day event that you grow to enjoy.

This particular Igue festival I attended was under the rulership of the late Oba Erediauwa N'Edo Uku Akpolokpolo, and I could recount the warm reception he granted me. Though it was a hectic day for him, the aura and charm with which he greeted everyone were a testament to the nature of the Benins.
We are diligent, proud, confident, resilient, and, above all, respectful of the people and things around us. This philosophy is embedded in our basic cultural norms and forms the foundation of our societal values. A Benin man would risk his life to fight for you if he felt you were threatened by something or someone, and he would do this without thinking twice.

To us, if you selfishly trade humans for guns today, you'll need more guns to protect yourself from internal strife tomorrow. A clear moral imperative, yes, but it was also a fiercely pragmatic approach to our way of living. This may be why Edo State has become one of Nigeria's most politically independent states today.

I believe this philosophical narrative was why we didn't enforce our language and customs in the many territories we conquered. As a tribe known to be fierce in war and one that conquered so many lands, it is a bit unsettling how we've been reduced to just a single state in present-day Nigeria. Our lack of indoctrination may have eroded the political leverage of the Benin people.

The British, despite all their flaws, knew the power of indoctrination, and they wielded it like a finely crafted sword to cut through the fabric of national identity in any territory they conquered. Echoing Muammar al-Gaddafi's words, "Nations whose nationalism is destroyed are subject to ruin." The British took this to heart, methodically erasing or diluting the sense of self of the nations they occupied. Nigeria was no exception to this rule.

Once they had political control, they set out to reshape the social and cultural landscapes. The introduction of Christianity played a pivotal role in this. Traditional African belief systems were labelled 'pagan' and marginalised, making way for the new Christian order. Not only did this afford the British moral authority—at least in their own eyes—but it also sowed division amongst the Indigenous people, casting aside centuries-old communal bonds and supplanting them with a foreign belief system.

But it didn't end there. The British were shrewd enough to realise that control extends beyond politics and religion. They began introducing elements of their culture—drinking coffee, smoking cigarettes, donning suits, and even advocating a new family structure centred around monogamy, contrasting with the indigenous polygamous systems. Every facet of life that could be "westernised" was, from architecture to education, and naturally, language. English became not just the language of governance but the benchmark for intelligence and sophistication.

In so doing, the British laid down a framework of lasting influence, a legacy that would endure long after they had packed up and sailed back to their lands. Their cultural, religious, and linguistic imprints had become so ingrained in the psyche of the colonised that they continued to dominate and shape the identity of these nations, Nigeria included, long after the end of colonial rule. And to be clear, many parts of Africa still dance to the tune of foreign-controlled capital and resources today.

However, our Obas, so preoccupied with integrity, avoided this path. Benin was a force in commerce, military strength, and art. Nevertheless, one thing the Benin Kingdom did not substantially engage in was the indoctrination of their conquered peoples. Sure, we imposed tributary systems and exercised military control, but the Benins stopped short of exporting their culture, language, and traditions to the annexed territories.

In contrast to the British, Benin's strategy was not centred on long-term cultural imprinting. Had it been, the Benin Empire might have been a dominant cultural and political force in contemporary Nigeria. The empire's influence could have extended beyond history, artefacts, and academic interest. We might be speaking a variant of Edo as a lingua franca in some areas of Nigeria, and the respect commanded by the Benins could be comparable to how English heritage is viewed globally.

But presently, that's not the case. The Benins were noble in their treatment of conquered peoples, but they missed out on the strategic opportunity to indelibly imprint their ideals, norms, and language onto the souls of those they ruled.

In hindsight, one could argue that the Benin Empire might have learned from the British approach. Had they undertaken a more systematic cultural and linguistic infusion in their conquered territories, the modern political arena could have looked markedly different. They might have wielded a geopolitical influence, rivalling even the largest ethnic groups in Nigeria today, such as the Hausa, Yoruba, and Igbos.

Yes, the British strategy was manipulative and exploitative, but it was also incredibly effective. As someone with a foot in both Western and African worlds, I can't help but wonder what a different sort of hybrid cultural existence we might have experienced had the Benins been as forward-thinking in the realm of cultural indoctrination as the British were.

This thought raises questions about how power sustains itself through culture and how legacies are built or dismantled. Although I find aspects of British colonialism abhorrent, I must acknowledge its cunning. It's cunning that the Benins, for all our glory, did not harness—and perhaps to our detriment.

Was a sense of pride preventing us from spreading the Edo language across our conquered territories? Perhaps we thought the magnificence of the Benin Kingdom spoke for itself—that we didn't need to enforce assimilation because the very air around the Oba's palace whispered stories of our might and benevolence. Maybe it was an underlying belief in self-preservation; perhaps we wanted the core of the kingdom, the heartland, to remain 'pure' in some way. But in the end, we paid a price. Our Obas, due to ignorance, focused on the moment and lost the long game.

Now, we are left struggling to reclaim our stolen oil wells with little to no political influence to effect the changes we wish to see. Past governments in Edo state have tried and failed. Why? Because Edo State, home of the ancient Benin Kingdom, is but one voice in the racket of ethnic influences that dictate the fate of Nigeria's natural resources. Despite its historical depth and richness, it lacks the political weight to tip the scales in a direction that would benefit its people specifically.

Compare this to the Yoruba, Igbo, and Hausa ethnic groups, each of which wields enormous influence on Nigerian politics owing to the sheer number of states they dominate. Their political heft affords them a voice that resonates in the corridors of power, a voice robust enough to secure natural resources and guide national policy to serve their interests.
This is the unfortunate reality of Nigerian politics: the greater your numbers, the louder your voice. This isn't merely about democracy; it's about power distribution.

Would things have been different if the Benin Kingdom had been more expansive, geographically and politically? Had we multiple states within the federation, akin to the Yoruba, Igbo, and Hausa? I dare say yes. The larger an ethnic group's representation in the federation, the more influence it wields in resource allocation. Size brings both visibility and viability in Nigerian politics.

Given the strategic missteps and what-ifs, one lesson stands out: the power of culture and education in defining and redefining power cannot be underestimated. Culture is not just a way of life; it is a strategy for survival, a tool for influence, and a pathway to immortality. Whoever controls a people's education and culture controls their narrative. And the narrative, as they say, is history itself.

The reality is that mistakes have been made, and our only hope of a miraculous revival as a state is education. How? Through indoctrinating our younger population and showing them their rich cultural history. Then, provide them with the tools they need to propagate our history, culture, and language in every geographical location they find themselves, just like the Yorubas are doing in Brazil, Cuba, Haiti, Peru, Jamaica, Puerto Rico, and the United States of America.

Yes, it will take time, but soon enough, more people, especially foreigners, will speak our language, love our culture, embrace our customs and side with us on matters that require a powerful voice and a massive population to decide.

If my Swiss mother could come to Edo State, learn our culture, and run a successful business for decades before she passed away, I see no reason why we cannot invest in education and export our culture, language, and heritage across borders.

O W Ọ R Ọ | 1 1

My first journey to Nigeria began on a cold Sunday, the 21st of December 1975, in my womb room at the Zürich International Airport in Switzerland. I was surrounded by a thrilling feeling of happiness and a paralysing excitement, which rendered time and its passing a slowly-paced torture.

My beautiful mother, Klara, was standing at the Swissair check-in counter with my elder siblings, Thomas and Barbara. If you are wondering what is happening, I am describing a story my mother and brother, Thomas, told me years later about the first time we came to Nigeria as a family. The only catch, however, is that I will be sharing this experience from my perspective, even though I was still a foetus when it all happened. A bit wild, you might think, but it is just how I have imagined it for decades, and although I would have wished to experience it live, I will invest all efforts in describing this story as though I was there, so do not get confused along the line. LOL.

On that day, my 6-year-old sister held her favourite doll dangling halfway to the ground with her right hand while her left was nestled gently in my mother's grip. I never really understood why she had to take her cracked and dirty no-eye doll along with her anywhere she went. You could see traces of countless stitches everywhere. My mother had carried out many surgeries on the doll to restore its defaults, being the doll doctor she was because my sister didn't want any other doll but the one she was holding.

Mummy, where are we going? my sister asked in Swiss German.

We are going to Benin City, in Nigeria.

Is that where daddy lives?

Yes dear

Will there be lions and elephants in his home and can I play with them? she

My mother, startled by her questions, couldn't hold herself back but burst out in laughter that drew the attention of passersby.

No, dear, certainly not, she replied.

My brother, standing to the left of my mother, remained grumpy. He was still trying to understand why he wouldn't be seeing his friends in Switzerland anymore.

At this point, my parents had been married for 6 years, and I'd been an occupant of this womb room for 6 months, which meant my rent was about to expire, and I would soon be thrown out into the realm of reality where only the toughest survive. In these past 6 months, I have noticed multiple rises in my mother's blood pressure due to various external factors. One of which I guess was my father. He spent most of his time outside of Switzerland, which was not beneficial to my mother in terms of support. She was alone most of the time with the kids. She had to manage, rearrange, and plan our upkeep with my grandparents and aunties while she was at work.
An event in the early winter of 1975 significantly impacted her. My father returned from his late shift at the Swissair base in Kloten. Because of heavy snowfall and no gritters, he could not discern the difference between the paved and unpaved roads. Due to this situation, he traversed kilometres of farmland and got lost. After much driving, he finally stopped his car in the middle of nowhere, stepped out, and looked over the area he was standing on. All he saw was snow. He looked back and saw a car with a siren in the distance. As the vehicle drew closer, he knew he might be in trouble.

Oh god! The police, He thought to himself as they approached him.

Good evening, Sir.

Both policemen greeted him as they drew closer to him on foot.

Good evening, officers.

We saw your tire marks when you diverged from the main road some fifteen minutes ago. You are currently on farmland, and we think you are lost.

Yeah, you are right; I am lost.

Prefect. We suggest you drive behind us. We will escort you back home.

Off they went, my father, flanked by a police car, and they arrived some 30 minutes later. The doorbell rang, and my mother opened the door. To her surprise, my father was standing beside two policemen. She stood there worried and speechless as her blood pressure rose. I could feel it. They later explained to her that her husband was lost and they were only doing the favour of directing him home. My mother asked them to come in for a cup of coffee as her usual way of showing appreciation, but they humbly declined and left.

As my father walked in, she closed the door behind him angrily. That night, they quarrelled about various pending issues.

I left with her the following day to get some groceries while my sister and brother stayed with my father. Amazingly, we were back after 2 hours, and the next thing we knew, we were in the kitchen preparing lunch. Because of the heavy snowfall, we spent most of the afternoon indoors.

At about four p.m., our house bell rang. My father opened the door, the same policemen who had directed him home just yesterday were standing outside.

Good afternoon, officers. Did I get a speed ticket? My father whispered.

No, nothing like that, sir.

Can we talk with you for a moment? they requested.

Of course, why not?

They informed him that his wife did not pay for the groceries she bought a while back, and the shop owner felt she did so unintentionally. My father, though unhappy with the news, was not really shocked as my mother had already displayed signs of dementia for some months before this incident occurred. He always knew her to be someone who hardly forgot to pay for something she bought, but with the latest signs she was showing and now this incident, he was worried about her condition, which we later found to be Alzheimer's. While it's hard to spot the early signs of Alzheimer's, cases are "marked by an uncertain starting point called Mild Cognitive Impairment (MCI). But while MCI might not always mean Alzheimer's is on the way, Alzheimer's very often begins with MCI. Maybe this event might have been an early indicator for my father to monitor his wife — if only he had kept track of all the slight declines that came up after this moment, maybe he would have been able to kick-start an early treatment for her.

He explained to them that she may have forgotten, and they gently requested that he discuss the issue with her to prevent it from happening again and fix a schedule to make the payment for the groceries. He thanked them and returned inside, shutting the door behind him.

My father stood there wondering and staring at my mother's bag. He opened the bag and verified how much was in her wallet. To his surprise, the money he gave her before we left for the grocery store was still intact.

When he closed the wallet and looked up, he saw her standing in the corner watching him. All hell broke loose; my mother's blood pressure fired up again, and they argued for over two hours.

A month after the incident, my father left Swissair for a new job in Benin City, Nigeria. He left immediately, hoping that we would all join him. Fortunately, my mother found a new job, too, in a retirement home in 'Büren an der Aare' just soon after my father left for Nigeria.

My mother worked as an experienced cook and hotel manager at the retirement home for 2 weeks before her boss called her into his office and told her some shocking news.

> *Please have a seat. I would like to inform you about some planned changes.*
>
> *Alright.*
>
> *The management has been planning a complete renovation of our facility and…*
>
> *Finally, this is fabulous. I am happy to hear this, my mother snapped in.*
>
> *Yes, they have finally fixed the date for the 1st of January. We plan
> to transfer all residents to a neighbouring facility, and will be
> closed for a year. We plan to resume in January.*
>
> *Wow, okay, this… this is long. So what are my prospects? my mother
> asked in a quavering tone.*
>
> *You resume with us in January. During this one-year closure
> period, I could apply for 80% financial support for 6 months for
> you. He offered,*
>
> *Thank you for your concerns. I think this won't be necessary. I will
> contact you in December to organise my reinstatement. She said as she made
> her way out of the office.*

With that news came the new future of a mother and three kids. The only viable option left for this brave woman was to go to Nigeria and make the most of what she had. It was one of the shortest decisions that my mother has ever made.

Now, back to the Swiss Air check-in counter. My mother presented all our passport documents, and in no time, she was handed all the boarding tickets needed. We made our way to the boarding gates. The boarding process was fast; soon enough, we were sitting on our outbound flight to Lagos, Nigeria. During pushback, I felt my mother staring outside the oval window as the plane took off. I felt her staring into the uncertain future that awaited her in Nigeria all through a flight that lasted six hours.

Awaiting us, in this far and unknown land, was my father at the airport in Lagos.

As the plane doors opened, we were greeted with a friendly wave of hot wind that spread an unforgettable scent of blooming nature mixed with a pint of petrol. As I have learned through my mother, even though the perfume of nature is dominant in the Nigerian air, the scent of combusted gasoline is also an everyday companion of any tourist who has strolled through any of the major cities in Nigeria, especially the smaller ones.

My mother presented our passports for verification by the customs officer.

Madame, is this your second time in Nigeria? the customs officer asked.

Yes, it is.

Wonderful! Welcome home.

My mother has always been a self-organising unit. She originated from a classic Swiss farmer's household and remained industrious, practical, and simple. She was nothing like Margery Michelmore, who had an immediate primitive insight into Nigeria and Nigerians after her brief stay. My mother may appear innocent and soft, but she actually had a side of her that remained a mystery.

Our meeting with our father at the airport was dramatic, and the ambience was so weird that any onlooker would think we hadn't known each other all our lives.

Getting to the arrival hall, my father was nowhere to be found. Some time passed before we suddenly saw a 4-footer (not sure about my father's height) hurtling towards us with a wild smile and open arms spread in an embrace. Of course, my mother was pissed, and of course, this act of familiarity took me off guard. Only after a long while did I realise that It had been my father's way of creating a psychological balance between the people he cared for. We entered my father's Volvo 264, then drove off to a hotel where we would spend the night before departing for Benin City the following day.

Arriving in Benin City by road from Lagos was a three-hour trip on well-tarred Nigerian roads. We halted en route for about an hour to have a late lunch and drinks. On arriving in Benin City, my father drove straight to Ikpoba Hill. We were going to be staying in a temporary place as our house was not yet completed. Our first steps into our temporary home were accompanied by an aura of singing. To our surprise, my grandparents organised a little welcome party.

Fully settled in, Thomas and Barbara had now started schooling, and my parents were en route to the University of Benin Teaching Hospital for my mother's monthly checkup; my house rent was almost due, and the doctor was just making sure that all was in place. After our hospital visit, we continued to Thomas and Barbara's new school. Barbara and Thomas were very nervous as they couldn't speak English. I mean, the only language they knew was Swiss German, only God knew how they adapted.

It was around nine p.m. in the morning of May 1976, and I began feeling really uncomfortable in my womb room. Could it be that my rent had finally expired? I guess these were the thoughts of my mother as she began screaming.

> *Oh my god, what are these sudden movements that I can feel within? she screamed out as she reached for the phone to call my father.*

The phone call didn't last long, as my father immediately called on Joseph to assist my mother in the hospital. He couldn't come himself because he had mixed feelings that morning. He was a bit confused and stressed simultaneously, so he was scared he would commit some blunders if he came up himself. Instead, he sent Joseph to help handle the situation. It was a rough start to a day at the office for him.

Joseph arrived a few minutes after the phone call and located my mother with the sound of her groan. With his help, we were on the next available vehicle headed for the University of Benin Teaching Hospital. Unfortunately, all the resident doctors were on a 5-day strike. Apparently, they wanted an end to unpaid financial entitlements, casualisation of medical officers, and poor job descriptions for interns in the hospital. Because of the strike, we were stranded outside the main hospital entrance. At this point, I could feel how stressed my mother had become in a country she hardly knew, with a political system broken just sixteen years into its independence.

Luckily, we were able to find help, and in 40 minutes, I woke up to the pungent smell of hospital disinfectant invading my nostrils. The room was silent apart from my heavy breathing, my mother's screaming, and the beeping sound from the Holter monitor. I slowly opened my eyes, squinting in an attempt to sharpen the blurred images before me. I glanced around and saw the deserted, blue and white-themed hospital bedroom. How long have I been here? I shut my eyes, trying to remember what had exactly happened. Then it all hits me with a bang. The memory of it all starts to occupy my thoughts. My nine busy months are now over. My rent had finally expired.

> *How's the baby? I hope he is okay?*

> *Yes, madam, he's fine, and congratulations, it's a bouncing baby boy.*

> *I don't really care if it's a boy or a girl; all I want is for my baby to be healthy.*

> *Well, yes, he's fine, he reaffirmed.*

After my birth, everything changed. The plan changed. My mother decided early not to return to Switzerland anymore. My mother was convinced that things could be achieved in Nigeria, particularly in a village called Benin City. She created a draft plan of business ideas with my father. The first implemented plan was the furniture company, which started in 1982 and is still in operation today. The second was her bakery by the name of Uphill, where she made a famous Swiss bread called "Zopf". I later rebranded it as "Mummy's bread" because I could not pronounce the word.

My mother's bakery was doing well until a bitter trade dispute between the United States and Nigeria over wheat imports posed a tough challenge for local Nigerian producers. The then-ruling president of Nigeria wanted to increase domestic food production by banning the importation of wheat. When the ban on wheat was effective in 1987, there were no more prospects for producing locally grown wheat. This automatically discouraged wheat consumption in Benin City and Nigeria as a whole. My mother was forced to close her bakery because of this poor policy by the then Nigerian government.

As I can recall, our daily childhood routines were mainly about my mother spending most of her time grooming and educating us while my father was busy at work. I would usually jolt out of bed at the sound of my name and rush into the toilet to brush my teeth.

At home back then, our names were yelled out in chronological order, and being the youngest meant I always had more "sleep time". The smell of thyme and white pepper wafting from the kitchen meant our house help was almost done with the classic Nigerian omelette.

We usually ate our omelettes with bread from my mother's bakery ('mummy's bread'), but now we had to make do with bread we bought from a nearby kiosk. Most days, we scarf our breakfast down quickly with boiled yams before piling into the family Peugeot 404 with my mother, which we pronounce "Pee-Joe."

We would greet our family driver, Mr Joseph, in unison as he drove us to school. On our way, my mother would purchase newspapers from the road.
"Come here!! You get Punch or Guardian?" she would ask in pidgin to a racing newspaper vendor racing after our car in heavy Benin traffic. Balancing a stack of newspapers on his head with a few stuffed underneath his left armpit, the vendor skilfully pulls out a punch and exchanges it for 1 Naira.

Our morning commute takes us to Ugbowo, a suburb of one of the many agglomerations that collectively make up Benin City. Barbara, Thomas, and I would spill out and run through the gates of our primary school, just in time for morning assembly, as students gathered in the red-dusty yard to sing the Nigerian national anthem. I stand in the yard, watching as my mother steps back into the car and drives off.

During the lunch break, I usually grabbed a meat pie, scotch eggs (boiled eggs coated in minced sausage mix and fried), and a bottle of cold Coca-Cola. I devoured everything in no time and ran off to play football with my friends. We would form a ragtag team of kids and play various games together.

When it was five p.m., the school bells would ring, indicating it was time to go home. My mother was in the factory most of the time; hence, Mr Joseph did his usual tour by picking up my sister and brother before me. After navigating late rush hour traffic, we arrived at a hearty lunch dinner prepared by my mother. We usually ate separately from my father, who usually enjoyed his dinner in front of the television.

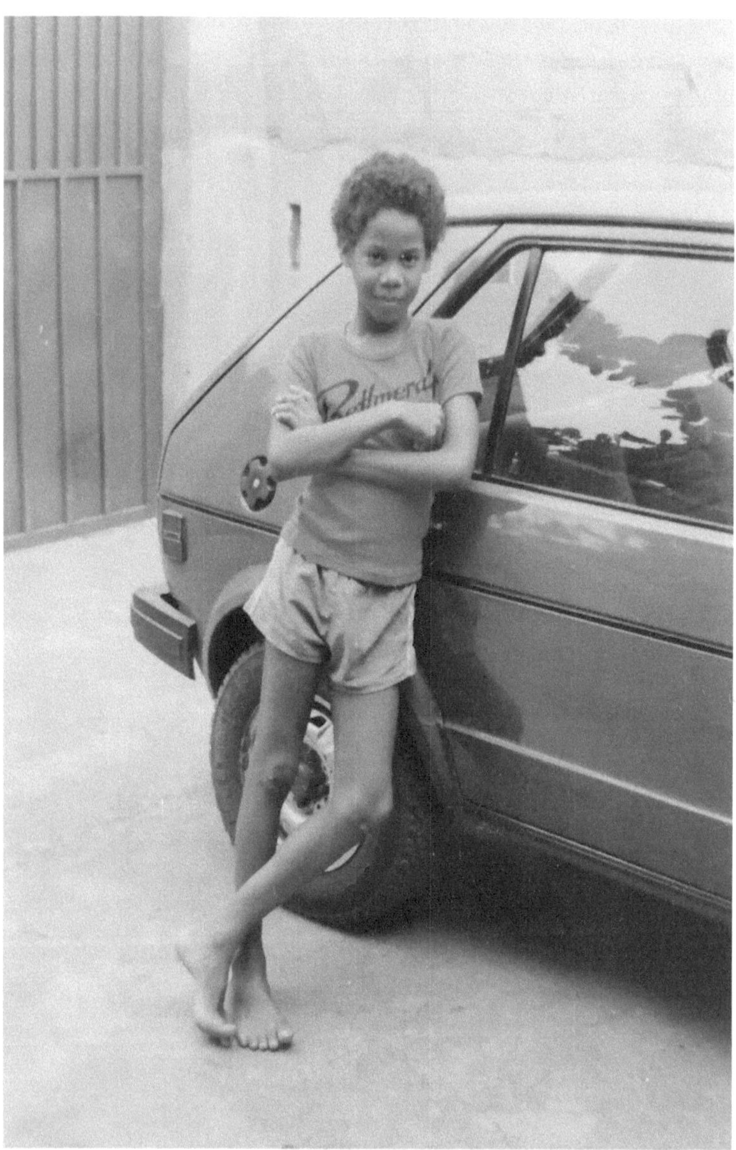

I W E V A | 1 2

It was ten a.m., and I was in Paris en route to Nigeria. I arrived at the Charles de Gaulle Airport in plenty of time—enough time to eat breakfast in the lounge before heading to my gate—but I almost missed my flight to Lagos altogether because of an absolutely amateur and boneheaded move. I waited until the last minute to leave the comfy lounge and head to my gate, wrapping up the last pieces of scrambled eggs on my plate.

Arriving at the gate, the passengers lined up at the door in stanchioned-off lines labelled A, B, and C for boarding groups. I had a C, so I found the appropriate line and waited my turn. The line didn't even move for about twenty minutes, and when I finally made it to the agent taking tickets, I came to the shocking realisation that I was in the line for the flight to Timbuktu, Mali. All the Lagos passengers had already boarded through the gate next door, just a few metres away. I panicked as I ran over to the correct door; thankfully, I made it through the jetway and onto the plane as the last passenger (yeah, I was that guy) with just minutes to spare. How I would have absolutely hated myself for missing the flight to Nigeria!

One of the few things I've noticed about myself is that I prefer air travel to other means of transportation. Growing up, my mother often told me how excited I was when we were on a plane. Back then, we travelled annually to Switzerland for Christmas or school holidays. My favourite moment is usually the pushback! I just love the feeling.

We landed at Murtala Muhammed International Airport in Lagos a little before seven p.m. on schedule. My trips to Nigeria are usually accompanied by thoughts as soon as the plane touches down. Hope and expectations begin to emerge from nowhere. I've always wanted to see a better Nigeria or a Nigeria that is progressing. I'm always hoping for a wow effect when I return to the country, perhaps because it has been a while since I last visited, and I probably still have a bit of patriotism. Unfortunately, as soon as I stepped out of the plane, my hopes were immediately crushed by the sight of a jet bridge that was in a deplorable state.

My first stop was the health officer, who asked to see my yellow card; thank goodness I had it on me. The immigration queue area was a 50 by 50 hall room with airport-style waiting seats, two large wooden desks behind which two immigration officers sat, and two of the four sides were glass with views of the main immigration area and baggage claim. So I walked up to one of the big wooden desks where my documents were inspected, and my passport was stamped. The lady seemed impressed that I was a carpenter (I had to declare my occupation on the entry form), and she asked about my job and some Swiss chocolates before welcoming me to Nigeria with a smile.

Upon entering the arrival hall, a woman in uniform approached me and asked if I needed a taxi. I replied, "No thank you, I have someone picking me up."
I picked up my bags and went outside the terminals and down the sidewalk. As soon as I saw Teddy, I was relieved. He assisted me in getting my bags into his black Toyota, and we headed home to his apartment. We departed for Benin City on a locally operated flight the following day. I didn't have much time to spend in Nigeria since I switched jobs back in Switzerland.

The main reason I was in Benin was to spend some time with my parents, especially my mother, who I was told was ill. As soon as I arrived in Benin at about eleven a.m., we took a taxi to my parents' home. The streets were still flooded from last night's rain, so Teddy and I had to step over various pools of water before arriving at my home.

Rat-Tat-Tat… I knocked on the gate.

Who is that? the security man asked as he moved to open the gate;
both Teddy and I kept silent as he swung the door open.

Ha! Oga, welcome sir, good afternoon, he greeted excitedly.

Hello Aboki, thank you. How you dey na?

I dey fine, Oga! he replied.

Okay, where are my mother and father?

Madam dey inside, but Oga just newly comort now go factory.

Alright, na. I go say make dem bring something for you later.

Thank you, Oga. God bless, he said as he danced around in joy.

I and Teddy proceeded to the main sitting room, and just as we were stepping in, Bola walked in on us.

Stefan, welcome!!! she shouted out in excitement.

Ahh, my dearest Bola. Good afternoon, dear. How are you?

I am fine and so glad you're back. Your mother has been calling your name from time to time.

Where is she?

She is upstairs. She has not been feeling well today.

I immediately climbed upstairs with Teddy to meet my mother. We found her lying on the sofa.

Ahh Stefan, you're back. I am so happy to see you, she greeted me excitedly.

My dearest, how are you feeling now?

I am okay. Don't worry too much.

Are you sure? Because Bola told me you weren't feeling well.

Don't mind her, my dear. I'm fine, and I'm getting better, she said as she adjusted herself to an upright position so she could go through the stuff I had bought for her.

I got her a rectangular block of Gruyére Cheese, some panadol tablets, some Nescafé Gold de Luxe packs, a small bag of curry paste, a small refillable pack of Knorr Aromat and some Swiss potatoes. I could see the excitement in her eyes as she went through the things I brought. She even requested that the Nescafé Gold de Luxe coffee be made for her immediately. Teddy and I sat quietly as she consumed her coffee slowly; my heart broke as I saw my precious mother fading right before my eyes.
I later learned from Bola that my mother had been showing signs of dementia, and she even sometimes forgets important details. She quietly explained the situation to me and Teddy.

Osaigbovo! my father called out.

I guess he learned from the security man that I was back. I immediately went downstairs to join him while leaving my mother in Bola's care. Teddy opted to stay with Bola while I went to meet my father. He suspected we were about to have a family discussion.

Lagiesan, I greeted.

Hello, son, I see your trip was okay.

Yes, sir.
It seems you have seen your mother already and heard of her ill health?

115

I sat there dumbfounded; I couldn't even lift a muscle, "what I'm hearing cannot be true," I thought to myself. The rest of my few days left in Benin were dedicated to my parents, trying to resolve the reality of my mother's illness. I researched treatment centres in Benin and Lagos but found nothing, and just before I left, I concluded with my father and elder siblings that it was best we brought her back to Switzerland.

2 months after I returned, my sister ensured she was moved from Benin to join us in Switzerland. My father assisted in making all the preparations for her definitive departure from Nigeria. The fact was, the news of my mother's dementia diagnosis struck us unexpectedly. From the point we learned of her illness, our lives changed forever because she was the cement composite holding our family together. She was the one that always had a solution for everything.

When my sister finally brought my mother to Switzerland, we agreed that my mother would spend some months with me in my house in Bümpliz in the city of Berne.

During this time, my mother underwent various medical checks. I spent most of every day with her when I was not working. My two sons, Femi and Seyi, visit me every 2 weeks. With my sons around, I was running two households, especially when my mother's dementia progressed. I needed to make her meals, deal with her washing, put her to bed and get her up in the morning. Fortunately, Spitex Home Care Services, an institution that provides nursing care at home, supported me during this long and painful phase of my life.

My mother and I were always very close, and she became a loving grandmother to my children. She had been a wonderfully selfless character all her life, always helping others with her lovely sense of humour and creative intent. She was a perfect artist, full of power and wisdom.

While she was with me, I tried often to make her laugh, but with every sunrise, it was getting much harder. Although there were still little signs of self-awareness in her that made her respond to some of my jokes. There was this particular time she lifted her fists in anger but dropped them suddenly and said, 'No, I don't do that, do I?' I said, 'No, you don't. That's not you.' This made her laugh afterwards, and even I joined in on the laugh that lasted for some seconds, but I would have done anything to make them last forever.

I made her laugh on a specific weird occasion with one joke I made relating to when I was a child. It was four a.m. when I heard my apartment's front door squeaking. I stood up and rushed to the front door. To my surprise, the door was open! I went to my mother's room only to find my father sleeping comfortably and my mother nowhere to be found. I returned to the front door in panic mode and went downstairs. There, I saw my mother in her pyjamas, barefoot, trying to open the main house door.

> *Mother, where are you going? I asked as I observed her struggling to*
> *open the door with trembling hands.*

She told me she was going to the market, not just any other market, but the Ikpoba Hill market in Benin City, Nigeria. Shocked by her response, I gently guided her back upstairs to my apartment. The whole experience lasted about six minutes. As we entered my apartment, I helped her sit at the kitchen table while preparing two cups of hot tea. I also went to her room to get her a pair of wool socks.

As soon as I was done preparing the tea, I served and watched her as she gradually sipped from it. "Thank you for this," she said with a smile as she sipped from her cup. The idea of cracking her up with a joke came to mind there.

> *Mother, remember how you brushed my teeth when I was younger?*
> *You were sometimes a bit hard and I would run away and you would chase*
> *after me as if it was a police-catch-thief operation.*
> *Do you still remember those days?*

She burst out in laughter and said,

> *That's not true, Stefan. That's certainly not true, she said as she*
> *continued laughing, almost spilling the tea in her hands.*

I watched closely as she sipped her tea and laughed when she remembered the joke I had told occasionally. Moments of cheerful banter like this were rare, but they helped me feel that the mother I knew was still with me.

Our family's experience with dementia is like that of many other families. We juggled my mother's long-distance care with Spitex and some helpful neighbours for 2 years. Things deteriorated with some of the neighbours over time, and the police were called in on a particular incident that remains fresh in my mind.

One disastrous weekend, my mother slipped into the washroom in the cellar and collected all the clothes from the washing machine. This led to my neighbour, Hans, informing the police of a theft that took place. The police came into everyone's apartment to search for the clothes. I remember that day like it was yesterday. I had just come back from my run. Seconds later, the bell rang. I opened the door to find two policemen and Hans standing with a firm, frowning face.

Good evening, sir, one of the policemen greeted.

Good evening; how can I help you?

A theft was reported three days back, and we are here to search through all the apartments. Here is the warrant for this building!

Hmm. Okay, what was stolen?

A bag of clothes.

How many people are living with you? the police officer asked as he peered into my apartment.

Just me and my parents. Please come in, I replied, stepping aside to allow them to complete their search.

The policemen walked in and started their search.

Abeg, shine your eye Stefan, them be 419, my mother said jokingly in pidgin.

The policemen and my neighbour didn't understand what she meant, but I laughed hard, as my mother had just made a real Nigerian joke about the Nigerian criminal code.

I proceeded to ask my father if he had heard or seen anything regarding the missing clothes in the last few days, and he replied,

No.

So, I was kind of confident the missing clothes were not in our apartment.

The policemen searched the kitchen, went to the toilet, and then went to the sitting room. I had 2 cupboards in there. The police officers opened the cupboard with some 18th-century drawers that belonged to my grandfather. There, they saw a strange green bag. Suddenly, my mind started travelling.

Hmmm, whose bag is this? one of the police officers asked.

Before I could react, Hans shouted, That's my bag!

The police requested I fill in a statement form, which they gave me to explain why the bag was in my possession. The situation was cleared up within a day after I supplied the police with a signed health statement from our family doctor regarding my mother's condition. The most inspiring part of this experience was that after that day, Hans checked on my mother occasionally to see how she was coping. Hans even went the extra mile to take my mother for late afternoon walks.

I remember vividly when Klara's mother's (my grandmother's) twentieth burial anniversary was approaching, and I decided I would take her to her mother's resting place. After lunch, I put her in her coat, gloves, hat, and scarf and let her sit on her favourite spot in the kitchen while I tidied it up. After the brief cleanup, I suggested we leave shortly for a walk, and she came gladly.

I grabbed my car keys, and we approached the garage. I opened the front passenger door and helped her into the car, where she sat comfortably. She tried her best to keep me entertained with various self-discussions and observations, but the conversation made little sense to me with every kilometre I drove.

When I got to the cemetery, I parked the car about forty metres from the entry gate at the foot of the slope.

> *Ah, we are going to visit my mother. She said excitedly as we approached the hill.*
>
> *Yes, mother, it is her memorial day. I replied.*
>
> *Ahh, you are a fantastic son. I love… she mumbled without completing the sentence.*

Though she didn't complete the sentence, I was dumbfounded by her intentions, and to be frank, I can't exactly describe the emotions that took over my heart that day.

As we sat on a metallic wooden bench together, she grabbed my hand. For the next couple of minutes, we sat silently as she looked over her mother's resting place.

My mother lived with me for 4 months before she was finally transferred to a home. During these months, the following capturing interactions were engraved in my heart:

The fun times came when we had to shoo the goats out of the bathroom because they were keeping her awake. The bad times were when she didn't recognise me for days and the devastatingly sad days when she would introduce herself and ask my name. The times we argued as we tried to exist in her world while she struggled to exist in ours, and the nights when I would sit, rocking her in my arms.

I realised my mother was my superhero just by perceiving how fulfilling and prosperous her life was.

The day I feared finally came, and it was time to take her to a new home. She got up early that day and was already sitting on her favourite sofa. I walked in and found her sitting quietly and staring at the window. I closed in, sat beside her, and held her hands as I tried to communicate, but she didn't understand what I was saying clearly. My father later joined us as we prayed together as a family before commencing our journey to her new home.

I W E H A | 1 3

It was Friday, January 7th. Teddy, a whiz in social media consulting, and I had just touched down in Lagos for the first leg of my journey back to Switzerland. We were en route to meet Frank, the barber who was a staple in Teddy's neighbourhood.

Teddy often sang Frank's praises with so much enthusiasm. "My guy, if my barber touch your hair, eh?" Teddy once said, "You sef go trip for yourself when you jam mirror."

To call in his bragging, I took a bold step of faith and tried out the so-called celebrity barber he was hyping nonstop. As soon as we got to Frank's barbershop, we met some other men there, and they were discussing football teams, bashing each other's clubs and analysing the peculiar intersection of tribal and football politics.

The idea of being an Edo man who doesn't watch football is already a funny topic to the average Nigerian, but being an Edo man that supports West Ham is nearly unimaginable, and I was in both categories. I am not a huge fan of football, though I watch some games occasionally. Plus, I support West Ham United. I have been a semi-fan of the club since I was a child. The good thing is, I didn't let anyone at the barbershop know any of these details during the banter, or else I would have been roasted.

Our conversation at the barbershop morphed into a pointed critique of Kenyan Manchester United fans. The gist was so funny that I had to record it on my phone. I enjoyed every bit of it.

During the gist, I decided to get a haircut. I was so absorbed in the conversation that I hardly noticed Frank working his magic. When he finally finished, I squinted into the mirror, my glasses back in place. My reflection revealed the finest haircut I'd had in ages. At least Teddy was right for once, LOL.

Frank had innovatively styled my beard, leaving a subtly refined moustache, and the side fade was simply impeccable. Just as I was about to leave the chair, Frank stopped me, insisting he wasn't finished yet. He then treated me to a luxurious steaming facial towel treatment. It was simply sublime.

Later, some of Teddy's pals dropped by, and we ordered dinner from the food vendor just outside the shop. Over a hearty meal of Suya and chips, we swapped stories about our unforgettable school experiences.

Suddenly, Teddy nudged my shoulder. "Bros, we need to dey go. Tomorrow na early day for us." We rose, went to Teddy's car, and called it a night.

It's unbelievable how swiftly time passes by. It's been 7 long, emotion-filled months since my mother departed this world. The constant ache of her absence never truly eases. Yet, here I am, back on the road, transitioning through Amsterdam, en route to Switzerland.

I arrived at Basel Airport, Switzerland, lost in reflection, as I sauntered towards the luggage carousel. My 3 most recent trips to Nigeria were unforgettable, the most recent being my encounter with Ayo. I couldn't help but think about him. Did he make any sales today? Were his feet aching from his relentless run amid the notorious Lagos traffic?

I powered on my mobile, my gaze fixed on the little icon in the upper right corner. As my service provider automatically searched for a 5G network, I continued to mull over my thoughts.

I can still remember my encounter with Ayo during a Go-Slow traffic jam along Ikeja, Lagos, while returning from one of my many trips from the airport. Ayo, one of thousands of roadside hawkers, immediately caught my attention because of what he was selling and, later, his insightful and mature character. He was selling Walter Disney characters. Stuck in traffic, he approached my window and said,

Oga, abeg buy Walter Disney characters for your pikin!

I rolled down my window and teased him,

Who tell you say I get pikin?

Oga, I see some white beards for your moustache, you too fine.
Man like you, you don collect woman, no be market you dey
again!

I burst into laughter, marvelling at how he had analysed me in a few minutes. Playing along, I responded,

Na, true; you talk so!!!

Yes oga, look, I get Dumbo, Cinderella and plenty more for my bag… pick two, you go pay for one.

Teddy, who was beside me, was laughing heartily. Intrigued by Ayo's energy and wit, I asked,

Who be Walter Disney? Im name nor be Walt?

No oga, na American animation artist im be, and im real name na Walter!

Hmmmm, you sabi! How old you be, and wetin be your name?

Oga, I be 16 years old and my name na Ayo.

All this time, Ayo had been running beside our car at a pace of about 4 kilometres per hour. Suddenly, traffic eased up, and our car started moving faster. He had to sprint to keep up. I asked Teddy if he could pull over, which he did, to my surprise.

After we parked beside the road, I exited the car and waited for Ayo, who arrived a couple of minutes later, panting heavily.

Ayo, I wan ask you three questions. If you fit answer two correct, I go buy something from you.

Aiiii Oga, no wahala, ask me!

First, who be Queen Idia?
Second, who be Kanta Kola?
Third, when dem abolish slavery?

Teddy grumbled beside me,

Stefan don turn history teacher sef.

Ayo started laughing, scratching his head a few times before responding.

To tell you true, I know small thing about Queen Idia..

Go on, Ayo, na he or she?

Dem dey call am the mother of the Benin Kingdom. She be warrior. You fit see her mask with her famous headdress everywhere.

Not bad, Ayo. What about the other two?

Oga, I never hear about dem before…

I touched my beard, contemplating his response. Then, I said,

But you don hear about slave trade before?

Yes, oga, na that time when white people carry us go help dem work for their lands…

Help dem work for their lands?!!!

Yes, oga.

Part of wetin you talk dey correct, but the other part no correct.

Oga, why you dey ask all these questions?

Because I see you dey sell Walter Disney items, I wan know if you sabi where you come from. I fit tell say you be Yoruba person, abi?

Yes, oga.

Who be Ọsanyin?

Aiiii Oga, that one easy na, ohh. Im be the òrìṣà of herbs, forest, and medicine. Na my favorite spirit be that!

Good job, now I dey happy. Where your mama and papa dey, and why you no dey school this time?

Oga, na long story, but I go cut am short; my papa leave my mama. To pay our house rent, we all dey work to support my mama.

Na true? How many children your mama get?

Four, oga.

Chai.

Teddy whispered in my ear,

Abeg, round up, hunger dey catch me. I nodded,

I don hear.
Okay, Ayo, I go pay for 2 Cinderellas.

Oga, thank you very much, I dey very grateful. I dey accept cash

or card.

I burst into laughter after hearing this.

Wetin? you get Point Of Sale (POS)?!!

Yes, oga, na my mama account for FirstBank of Nigeria.

Okay, but I go pay cash. I handed the cash to Ayo.

Thank you very much, oga. I dey grateful. Here are your characters.

I dey insist make you keep them.

But oga…

No wahala. Also, take this cash for transport.

I handed Ayo a slip with an address written on it.

Meet us for this place by five p.m. today. Nor come late oh.

Okay, oga, I go come.

Teddy drove off as I said goodbye and got back into the car. I watched Ayo from the side mirror. He was jumping with happiness. Ayo could have been my son! My heart ached.

Later that evening, just before five p.m., Teddy and I visited his favourite restaurant in Ikeja, Bukkahut. This marvellous establishment is known for its delectable Suya chicken, among other delicious offerings. Conveniently, the restaurant was just a five-minute walk from our rendezvous point with Ayo. As we sat on the veranda, we indulged in two generous servings of Suya with ice-cold bottles of Star beer.

Before we knew it, it was already ten minutes past five. Teddy immediately stood up to fetch Ayo, returning with him just ten minutes later. Ayo's face was beaming.

Good evening sir, I appreciate your kindness, Ayo greeted.

Hello Ayo, have a seat.

Thank you, sir.

So how was the rest of your afternoon?

Just the usual, sir. The hustle and bustle of Lagos.

As a waiter approached our table to take further orders, I turned to Ayo.

Ayo, are you hungry? Would you like something to eat?

That's very kind of you, sir. I think I would love to have some suya and a cold drink. That's all, he replied.

With Ayo's order taken care of, we could talk.

So, Ayo, I have something exciting in mind! You seem to be a very bright boy. How long have you been out of school?

Sir, about 2 years now.

Hmmm, would your mother be supportive of the idea of you going back to school?

Sir, I think she would, if she had the financial resources. She was a teacher herself and values education greatly!

Okay, I think we can find a way for you to go back to school. To do this, you will have to convince your mother. I would be willing to pay your annual school fees, and I would also provide support for your mother and siblings during your GCE period.

Ayo was speechless and excited. He jumped out of his seat, shouting, "Sir!! Is this really happening!!!"

I tried to reassure him,

Well, you seem to have a good heart, you are smart, and my son is just a year younger than you. I believe you should not be deprived of your basic needs.

Ayo was lost for words. Tears started streaming down his face.

But, I added, there is a catch. You have to send proof of your semester results and your project work, and I will organise the payments with the school directly myself. You will have to continue your hustle during the school holidays to support your mother. This is a chance for you. Don't mess it up!

Ayo remained speechless.

To plan the support for your mother while you are at school, I will transfer $75 per month. That's about $2.5 per day. With some parallel

> *side hustle, this should be enough to keep all of you going.*

Teddy whispered in my ear,

> *That's about 31,000 Naira (this was according to the exchange rate at the time). Security guards and cleaners start with 20,000, some get 30,000 to 40,000. I think this should be enough.*

Ayo remained speechless for a while. Soon, his Suya and drink arrived. I watched as his eyes sparkled like the morning star.

> *Enjoy your meal, Ayo. Meanwhile, could you give me the bank account details linked to your account?*

Ayo called out the account details, which I swiftly entered into my Nigerian mobile banking app to make the transfer.

A few minutes later, his phone rang. His mother's voice was loud, and a mix of joy and confusion echoed from the phone—joy because of the unexpected funds and confusion because she couldn't identify any of her products that would've resulted in such an amount.

As Ayo explained the situation to his mother over the phone, their cries of joy and confusion reverberated through the phone. It was an infectious moment, the exhilaration akin to when Nigeria won the Nations Cup. After passing my email address to Ayo and ensuring he finished his meal, we said our goodbyes and went our separate ways.

I had now arrived in Switzerland and at the airport. Just a few minutes after landing, I received over 15 messages from various friends in Nigeria, all checking to see if I had arrived safely. Nigerians are practically my brethren; they are among the most amicable, friendly, genuine, and fun people I know. Their friendliness and openness might seem unusual to foreigners who have never been to Nigeria.

While walking the streets, markets, or malls of Nigeria, I often received compliments from complete strangers. "Looking good, brother!" they'd call out. Such overt warmth from strangers is something I've only experienced in Nigeria and Cuba.

The camaraderie extended to gatherings with my friends, where the highlight would often be sharing stories peppered with playful cussing and laughter. I relish our jokes about Nigerian schools, parents, Benin spiritualists, and, notably, Buhari. These never fail to brighten my day.

My trip was a success, and as I collected my luggage and exited the airport, I felt a pang of nostalgia. While I was waiting for the bus, my wife called.

Hey, love, welcome back home. How was your trip?

Thank you, dear; all went perfectly.

I'm thrilled to hear that. Naija na you-never-know country ohhh, she said, joking in her half-perfect pidgin, causing me to burst into laughter.

Yes, there is truth in your remark. So, what's new?

Body dey inside cloth; I can't complain. I was just put on a Cuba rotation. I'm leaving in three days...

Speaking of the devil, I chimed in, I was just thinking about Cuba before you called.

Oh wow. Well, I'm waiting for you at home.

Okay. I'm on my way now dear, take care.

When I think of Cuba, the word that instantly comes to mind is "charming." Despite my unfavourable encounters with various officials, such as police officers and customs officers, I've always been drawn back to the country's charm.

Fast-forward to a few days before my potential trip to Cuba. I was on 'standby,' meaning I would only board if there was enough seat space. I packed, unpacked, and repacked my baggage in anticipation.

The day before my departure, I found myself at the Zürich Airport's main hall with my wife. We parted ways as she left for her debriefing. Back then, she was a flight attendant for Edelweiss, one of the international Swiss carriers. Edelweiss's positive work ethic and lifestyle reminded me of Swissair from my childhood days. The optimism was palpable.

Don't be late at the boarding gate, love. See you at pushback, she said, blowing a kiss as she departed.

I stood there, smiling like a Cheshire cat, watching her leave before calling out, "Aye, Captain!"

I proceeded to the Swiss check-in counters and patiently waited until my turn. The polite young man behind the desk took my passport, checked my details, and announced,

Good day, Mr. Asemota. Welcome on your flight to Cuba.

Thank you, I replied, and he handed me my business class boarding pass.

Before leaving the counter, I received directions to the Swiss Business Lounge, located past the security checkpoint.

My next stop was the grocery store, where I purchased fresh fruits for the entire Edelweiss crew. Having passed security and customs checks, I took the metro to my terminal, arrived, and promptly located my boarding gate.

As I sat there, legs jittering with nerves and anticipation, I keenly awaited the call for my name. When it finally came, my heart leapt. "Yes, yes, I'm in! Cuba, here I come!" I whispered to myself.

Approaching the boarding desk, I said,

Good evening, I am Asemota.

Good evening, Mr. Asemota, the attendant greeted me, We are happy to inform you that you can join us for this rotation!

Ecstatic, I thanked her and handed over my travel visa and Swiss passport. After a quick verification, she returned them with a friendly, "Thank you, sir. Have a great flight!"

Settling back into my seat, I was smiling with the same excitement as a child on the verge of getting an ice cream treat. After what seemed like an eternity, the final preparations for flight WK77 were complete.

As I approached the aircraft, I took one last look at the terminal and noticed the changing clouds. Once aboard, the flight's chief steward welcomed me, and I passed on the bag of fruit intended for the crew.

You must be Mr. Asemota, she said.

Yes, I am. A little something for the crew, I replied.

Scanning the interior, I caught sight of my wife at the end of the hallway, her smile radiant. Even in a crowd, she always spotted me first. Once settled into the plush comforts of my business class seat, I felt the aircraft begin to ascend. The slight rumble under my feet was a familiar part of the process - the retraction of the landing gear. Throughout the flight, I revelled in the impeccable onboard service. My wife, busy with the trainee under her charge, caught my eye only occasionally. What was an eleven-hour flight felt like mere hours before the pilot announced our descent into José Martí International Airport.

"Hola, compañeros," I murmured with a smile, welcoming the new adventure ahead.

I W E N Ẹ | 1 4

On October 7th, 1886, slavery in Cuba was abolished by the Spanish crown, marking a significant advancement in history. A big moment, you would agree. But here's the thing: even though they stopped slavery, it didn't magically fix all the racism.

Cuba, like many places, bears the indelible marks of its past, and the shadows of discrimination still persist despite the well-intentioned abolition. Being of a brown complexion made me a target for this form of discrimination, but it also enabled me to blend in well with the Cuban population. In fact, as a Nigerian Swiss, I had certain advantages over my wife. I could "pass" for a Cuban on the streets, and my "Cubanness" was rarely questioned based on appearance alone. This was particularly advantageous but came with its downsides, and now that I was back in the country, I could only hope that things had gotten better.

As our Edelweiss flight WK77 rolled up to its parking gate, something unexpected happened. There was this lady who started yelling to be taken off the plane immediately. Her attitude rattled everybody on board, and you could easily tell by the "who is this weirdo" look on almost everyone's face.

Some tried calming her down, but she only grew more furious. I was not buying the stunt. We have been in the air for hours; why the drama now?

As soon as the lead flight attendant announced 'disarm your doors and cross-check,' this lady was already yelling at other passengers to get out of her way as she bodied some and made her way to the exit.

The Chef de Cabin approached the lady midway to resolve whatever issues she was facing, but this only worsened things. She was unwilling to engage the young man and yelled at him instead.

Please, get out of my way!

I was observing the drama from my seat, but as soon as the flight attendant close to me opened her assigned cabin door, old memories from my last trip to Cuba snatched my mind off the scene, and I soon found myself enjoying the cool air-breeze-like memories that I was breathing in.

My thoughts were interrupted by a voice yelling,

I have a broken leg; move aside now!

I quickly regained my consciousness and recognised the voice. It was the same lady who had been causing all the trouble since we landed.

Well, then say it gently! Why are you screaming at me? I yelled back in defence as I gently moved aside for her to move on.

Deplaning is a facet of travel that can get people very riled up. So, I understood what she may have been going through, although I did not like how she reacted to it; she could have done better.

I sat in my seat for a few seconds, then stood up and went to immigration. There were 10 or more immigration lines with only three people each, so it moved quickly. Back on the plane, the Edelweiss agents had passed up immigration forms I had already filled out, further expediting the process.

The line I chose moved slightly faster than the line the Edelweiss Crew members were on, but I got grilled by the immigration lady for a solid ten minutes. I thought for sure I would be pulled into the secondary line because not only was I having trouble understanding her questions, but she didn't like the face-capture biometric pictures she took of me and had to redo them several times.

At one point, she asked that I "step back" from the booth while she was about to handle some sensitive details on her computer about me. After a few minutes, she stared at me, looked back at the computer, and stared back at me. She then asked to take my face photo again before finally granting me leave to enter Cuba.

"Should I stamp your passport?" she asked. The question confused me at first. Was she expecting me to say no? What if I said no? LOL.

Well, fortunately, I said, "Yes, please." With a smile, she went on to stamp my passport. I said, "Thank you!" and was allowed through as soon as she was done. My wife and her colleagues waited for me on the other side for over five minutes, watching me sweat it out.

Entering the baggage claim area, I approached her, and we shared some conversations, mostly about why it took me that long to get through and a few jokes. While conversing and laughing, 2 security officers with badges approached us.

Is this man disturbing you? one of the security men asked.

I stood there perplexed and totally confused.

No, not at all! Why are you asking? My wife responded.

Do you know this man? the officer asked again without answering my wife's question.

Yes, I do! You haven't answered my question.

Cubans are not allowed to be with foreigners here, but wait a minute, you sound Dominican!

I had not said a word. I was boiling gradually, but my wife, on the other hand, was trying to catch her breath while laughing. So, I just relaxed and allowed them to talk without interrupting.

Well, this is my husband, and I still don't understand where this conversation is headed. She responded, this time sounding very Dominican, like she wanted to pass on a message.

There is something about my wife when she speaks Spanish. She has a settled Dominican accent, which is because she lived in Boca Chica for over a year, and it influenced her tongue.

As soon as she responded, the security officers were confused. They were probably wondering what an assumed Cuban (me) was doing with a Dominican-sounding lady.

I felt it was time to round it up and ease the tension. So, I pulled out my Swiss passport from my right pocket and gave it to the security personnel closest to me. He checked it, and a sudden shock appeared on his face. He then quickly passed the passport to his colleague, who, at the site of the front page of my passport, looked at me, perhaps to confirm if it was the same face.

"Should I show them my Nigerian passport, too?" I thought to myself, but this was not the right scene to do so, and it's quite difficult to know when I can pull my Nigerian or Swiss passports, though I usually travel with both. Travelling with my Nigerian passport in some countries can mean immediate deportation, as certain countries discriminate against seeing the lovely dark green colour.

So, I gave up on the idea and summoned the courage to use the little Spanish I knew.

To embody my wife's advice, how else can you react to a situation like this but with a chuckle and a head shake, saying that quintessential Cuban phrase, "Well, what happened was…" and going on to narrate your ordeal. Because there was nothing any of us could have done about the racial issue except readjust to the surprises that our travels had inevitably thrown at us.

After the whole security check incident, we took a deep breath and moved on with our plans. We collected our baggage and made it outside the airport, where the Chartered Pickup bus awaited the Edelweiss crew.

The trip to the hotel lasted about fifteen minutes. We arrived around seven p.m., and my wife checked us in and collected our room card. We initially planned on stepping out to grab a bite, but we ended up remaining in our room.

My wife was organising our bags for our departure the following day, and I was helping her out when we heard a loud knock on our room door.

I walked towards the door and opened it. To my surprise, two hotel security officers presented themselves with their badges dangling from their right shirt pockets.
My wife called out to me,

Who is it?

It is some security personnel again, I replied.

What?…why? She asked in a confused tone as she joined me at the door.

*You and the lady must come with us. The shorter of the two commanded
in Spanish.*

Why? I asked.

*This room is registered to a Swiss lady and a Swiss travelling partner. Are
you the Swiss travelling partner? he asked me.*

Yes, I am. Why does that bother you?

*Well, we seem to believe you are not. Please come with us to the director's
office for clarification.*

My wife and I stared at each other with that look of frustration as we grabbed our passports and followed them, smashing our room door behind us in anger. We walked behind the two security men as they led the way to the director's office.

Little did we know that we were about to experience a deracialised perspective firsthand. A deracialised perspective allows for the belief that "racial" equality and democracy exist.

Cuba's history of racism originated with colonial Spanish settlers and their subordinated African slaves. However, it was not until the Castro reign that redistributive social and economic reforms had a positive and measurable impact on the quality of life for Afro-Cubans. Today, racism is banned by law but still alive on the streets, and my wife and I were about to experience one of those moments.

We approached the door marked "oficina del director," and one of the security men knocked on it. We heard a harsh voice shouting,

¡Por favour, ingrese a la oficina!

We all entered the office, and the director himself was sitting at the corner behind a semicircle desk. He was seated with another man, whom I presumed was his colleague.

Cubans are not allowed to lodge in this hotel, and we believe you are a Cuban, he said in Spanish while staring directly at me.

You look more like a Caribbean Mulato than a Swiss. His colleague joined in while also staring at me.

I was boiling inside because of their discriminatory statements. How can they treat a hotel guest in this manner? This was racism and the worst I have seen of it.

I looked at my wife and saw the anger and frustration on her face. It was like she was thinking exactly what I was thinking.

Is there a new law written in the Cuban constitution that says no Cubans are allowed on their own soil?

I asked in Spanish, though my command of the language was rather rudimentary, and my vocabulary fell short of what I had hoped for, but I could see they understood what I was asking.

The security director stared at me hard, as if he were hoping to scare me. Maybe he thought I was actually a Cuban who was trying to start a human rights conversation with him. He pretended like he didn't hear the question.

Are you Cuban? Tell me right now! he commanded.

I stared at him for a while and angrily pressed my Swiss passport into his hands.

He flipped it open, and I could see the shock on his face. The 2 security men who brought us also saw the look on their director's face and decided to leave. They took permission from him and left. It was clear they did not want trouble.

My wife handed him her passport, too, and he checked it. He gave it back to her immediately while holding on to mine. I took out my Nigerian passport and handed it to his colleague, who checked it and passed it to him, too, to check.

But this ban you talk about, I believe it was lifted by Raul Castro some years ago, right? Then why are Cubans still being targeted? I asked.

Yes, the ban has been lifted, but only a few hotels have implemented it. We are very sorry for any inconvenience this may have caused you and we are willing to do anything to make it right with you and your wife, sir.

There is nothing you can do to make it right! my wife retorted at him (her Spanish was definitely better than mine).

We can upgrade you to a presidential suite for no added cost, ma'am."

We won't be needing any of that!

Señor? he asked while staring at me, hoping I would give a different response.

I agree with my wife; we do not need an upgrade, I responded.

He apologised again and handed me my passports. I looked at my wife and could see how exhausted she was, so I decided it was best not to start a human rights debate with the director's colleague. I thought it was curious, though, that he used the word mulatto to describe us. This statement provides a valuable insight into the Cuban "racial" paradigm because, through this paradigm, he linked us to a shared metaphor of transnational "race" that subsumed both culture and class. His simplicity of statement and the ease with which he positioned us together made me question the processes and dynamics of "racial" construction in Cuba.

The next day, we woke up and made our way through a downtown Havana neighbourhood without having breakfast. I wore shorts, slippers, and a T-shirt with Queen Idia embroidered on it, carrying a bulging knapsack over my shoulder. My wife wore an Ankara dress, which I thought was beautiful and quite appropriate for the weather.

During summer (July), the temperatures in Cuba can reach 38 degrees Celsius. But on this day, the sun was shining, and everything felt so good. As we approached the capital city of Havana, we went our separate ways as earlier planned.
My wife was attending a community service organised by a non-profit organisation, and I was headed to a cigar pilgrimage tour. She told me she had been assigned to a project that included practising conversational English with some Cuban youth and adults and working with some of the local women in creating crafts. So, I wished her fun as I made my way to my destination on foot.

While trekking, I could perceive a faint scent of guava floating around the street, and occasionally, I heard the distant roar of the sea drifting in through the line of trees. The scenery was exhilarating, and I could listen to almost everything on my way as I strolled, observing every corner I could.

Across the street, I could see two ladies getting their hair done on the sidewalk, and I could hear the laughter belts from a group of men huddled around a game of dominoes, cigars hanging from their mouths. I approached the men, greeted them, and asked if I could sit and chat with them. One of them replied, "Si." With the help of my little Spanish from Dualingo, plus various hand signs, we could trigger a discussion.

I was intrigued by the facial traits of one of the men. He seemed Chinese, but when I heard him speak, he sounded Cuban, a typical local with no accent. So I asked him if he had a Chinese background, and he introduced himself to me as Yat-Sen. He told me he lives in Havana's Barrio Chino (Chinatown). Yen-Sen described Barrio Chino as a Chinatown without Chinese. He added that this seemingly accidental migration had its roots, like much of American history, in enslavement.

As early as 1857, when African slavery was becoming less popular across Europe and the Americas, hundreds of thousands of Chinese workers were brought from China, Hong Kong, Macau, and Taiwan to work in the sugar fields. Legally, Chinese were classified as white and contracted to working periods of eight years, but their social reality was closer to slavery.

Yen-Sen concluded that none of his comrades spoke Chinese, and most had never been to China, yet they had a strong bond with their Asian heritage. He asked where I came from, and I told him I was a Nigerian Swiss.

He wanted to know what it was like to be a Nigerian Swiss, so we discussed that.

It feels great to be Swiss, I said to him.

I am adaptable, like the Swiss Army Knife. On the other hand, I have this entitlement mentality of an average Nigerian, which is topped by a sense of belonging. I and most of my fellow Nigerians want to enjoy all the benefits of developed societies but don't want to pay the price. Country-wise, Switzerland has attained its economic potential, and Nigeria is still far from it! Yet, I still think Nigeria could aspire to become the Chinese of Africa if we work towards it.

He laughed and asked, 'how?'

Well, because I believe Nigeria's future could be as bright as China's, filled with potential and opportunities. Nigeria is an important country and the largest in Africa. China is also an important country, one of the largest in Asia and second in the world. However, only recently have the 2 countries established a significant relationship. Ni…

So how does this population stat help your country become a world economic powerhouse? You know it takes more than just a large population to be an important country, right? he asked, interrupting me midway.

Yeah, I do. I am aware Nigeria and China are two regional giants, yet distant. Their relationship has been less than one might expect for two large developing nations for various reasons: history, missed opportunities, and rival relationships. Nigeria's burgeoning population, which by all projections will be approaching something in the neighbourhood of 500 million in a couple of decades, puts us on course to become the third largest nation on earth after India and China and, thus, will make up the primary impetus for our quest to become a powerhouse, in the community of nations.

He looked me straight in the eye as if to say,

You have not answered my questions yet. I understood what he meant.

Obviously, we do not need a prophet to tell us that this growth in the Nigerian population will do little to propel us to economic progress and global respect. We will inevitably require a seismic political, economic, social, and strategic shift in the global order to achieve these goals, which none of the superpowers will encourage or support. Nigeria as a nation must assess their position in the world and work on factors to emphasise our strengths and the opportunities we can leverage relative to the existing superpowers and other emerging powers.

I see what you're getting at now, he commented while nodding. But what factors can you work on to become an important country?

That's a good question. China and Korea have pursued aggressive initiatives with major investments in research and development, infrastructure, and educational capacity. Asia's share of global research and development investment in the past years has increased from around

30% to over 40 to 50%. China has gone up from around 10% to over 18%, making it the second-largest spender after the US. We can follow in their footsteps and invest in these areas as a developing nation, and we can even partner with them and learn from these two powerful countries. Can you see where I am going with this? I asked him to ensure he understood.

Sure, I think I understand your point now. You want Nigeria to gradually grow into a world powerhouse without tramping on the existing superpowers. That way, they will suspect nothing nor try to stunt your growth. However, I have yet to understand how Nigeria can start its race for world power supremacy. Do you have any suggestions on that? he said to me.

He was getting my point, and I did not need to overemphasise my position to him. This gladdened my heart and gave me more energy to continue the conversation.

Well, we can start by simply handling the basics, like providing water and electricity for the teeming youths. Establishing a presidential and ministerial council made up of respected scientists focusing dedicatedly on science, technology, and innovation. Investing in science, technology, and innovation programs to diversify the economy, and launching a national education reform focusing on innovation and entrepreneurship.

These ideas will help produce the next generation of scientists, engineers, entrepreneurs, and innovation leaders who will drive our growing population to become a respected global economic power.

But ideas and wishful thinking aside, despite our wealth and human capital, the Nigerian economy is primarily driven by the service sector, especially the telecommunication and entertainment industries, and oil extraction. So before Nigeria can achieve anything I have said, they need to restructure the economy, develop new infrastructure, enhance economic performance, and push for more remarkable societal change, which I do not see happening anytime soon." I concluded.

Well, you have a point there. Corruption and massive migration are still a common issue in your country. Am I correct?

Sure, these are some problems we face today. I would say Nigeria today is no longer a country but an embassy where everyone is waiting for their visas to run away to their colonial masters for survival, me included. We laughed for a moment as soon as I said that.

I could compare Nigeria and China to two imaginary lifeboats, I added with my half-refined Spanish, which I had to supplement with many hand gestures, but he understood what I was saying clearly and handed me a cigar he was puffing on.

Alright, go on, he urged me excitedly. I took a few drags and handed him the cigar.

Nigeria is the first lifeboat, adrift in the sea to nowhere. This lifeboat is rickety, yet packaged to the brim. There is no real captain in the saddle, just a committee of mediocres that sees to its affairs. Its misery gets bigger, and a disaster can happen soon. The passengers of this same lifeboat are famished, poor, disease-ridden and restive. Chaos caused many to fall overboard and become flotsams. I added.

What about China? he asked curiously, passing the cigar to me.

The second lifeboat depicts China, everything in contrast. It is well-decked, stocked, built to last, and well-maintained. This lifeboat has a safe number of passengers, and among them are certified captains. Half of the occupants of this lifeboat made a case for helping the poor that were swimming in their direction. They align with the Christian ideal of being our brothers' keepers. They thought of parting with food and medical supplies and even bringing them onboard. But the other half thought otherwise. I replied to him.

Yensen went quiet for a while and stared at the busy street in front of us. I assumed he was reflecting on what I had just said.

Now I see what you mean; the other half must have opined that China lends to the stranded poor countries—not as a lifesaver on humanitarian missions but for a different purpose—in the interest of China?

Yes. You get my point.

Ah. I see.

Yen-Sen was right. Though it may sound callous, charity is not in the equation of wealth gathering. I am utterly fond of the Chinese, and I like discussing with them to understand their ideologies. I always get that Eureka effect evolving from conversations with them. This lackadaisical indifference may feel foreign to many people, but it is one I have grown to love. Perhaps that is why the cultural sociologist Hofstede describes "uncertainty avoidance" as a critical dimension of culture that differentiates people around the world.

I bid goodbye to Yen-Sen and jumped into a tuk-tuk taxi as I rushed to my next rendezvous with Jose, who would be guiding me on the cigar pilgrimage tour. The tuk-tuk dropped me off at a large colonial-style facade painted in cream and brick-red, titled

"1845 Partagas Real Fabrica de Tabacos" in large, bold block letters. This building was a landmark in downtown Havana.

We began the tour almost immediately, and I was fascinated by the massive structure and genius architecture I witnessed.

As I entered one of the rolling rooms, I could hear a man speaking over an antiquated intercom, reading a story from 'Prensa Libre', a newspaper in Cuba. His voice crackled through the speakers mounted on the red-fading walls of the factory. I could see dozens of men and women intently listening to his words as they rolled cigars of various sizes and shapes on the wooden workbenches that lined the main room of the first floor of the building. The rollers bang their small metal knives on wood slabs as they shape and finish cigars. The noise from their chavetas accentuated the tinny sound of the reader's voice and blended perfectly with the pungent aroma of rich tobacco leaves. I guess that was the most intriguing part of the tour because, as soon as I was herded into the colour-grading room, I decided that was enough and left. I wanted to see the casing, stripping, selecting, and other processes that would have afforded me a better understanding of the hundreds of steps it takes to produce a handmade cigar. But unfortunately, that was not the case.

The downside of the tour was a lack of organisation and being overcrowded with ill-mannered guests. I definitely preferred the tobacco plantation I visited in Vinales. It offered stunning landscape views of luscious green fields and scenic mountains.

Arriving at the hotel around half past three, my wife was already waiting in the lobby with our bags. We had planned to depart for Cienfuegos by bus, and she looked very excited.

> *Hmm, you smell cigars; I guess you've been ranting about Nigeria with some locals. She teased.*

I laughed and was amazed by the accuracy. Well, she was my wife and knew me better than anyone else. We left the hotel to grab a taxi to take us to the bus station.

Within a few minutes, we were at the bus station and on our way from Havana to Cienfuegos, situated in the southern part of the island. We ran into a perfect demonstration of the cultural differences between high- and low-uncertainty cultures. Without any sign or warning, our bus came to a dead stop in the middle of a major highway. Why? Well, the highway was literally ripped up with construction, thick rocks, gravel, and a big hole. All of my fellow travellers reacted by asking, "What is going on? " or "How long are we going to be here?" anxiously looking out the window to see what the problem was.

Meanwhile, our Cuban driver was totally undisturbed by the delay. He pulled out a newspaper and lifted his feet to wait out the traffic jam. We had hoped he would later explain what happened, but he never did.

In the end, the delay lasted about half an hour, and we enjoyed it. During the wait, we watched a Cuban history documentary to learn more about the context of the sights we were seeing, and the cheers and applause from everyone on the bus proved that we were all having the time of our lives.

Finally, we arrived at Cienfuegos, also known as La Perla del Sur (Pearl of the South), located on the southeastern coast of Cuba. Carrying our handy travel bags, we made it to our host family, where we planned on spending the next few days. On arriving at their lovely home, they welcomed us with ground beef, which was served alongside rice and beans.

Ground beef is a main dish in Cuban homes. It comes with all the flavours from the slow-cooked, low-heat process. Our host prepared the dish with traditional seasonings, potatoes, and olives and soaked it in a tomato-based sauce.

Cuban food is very meaty and offers some amazing desserts. But creating the perfect rice and bean dish at home does take a little time. We appreciated the fact that our host took her time to deliver.

As we were all seated at the table to dine, I waited until the rice first separated and fell apart; likewise for the black beans. With time, the beans became almost like a stew with a smooth and creamy taste, which was delicious. We spent the next two days with our hosts and enjoyed various local highlights with them.

On the third day, we departed early in the morning to visit the small and charming municipality of Palmira. This municipality is known for its Santeria brotherhoods, which are unique in this region, as well as for its rich and rural Yoruba culture. The culture of Palmira is very peculiar for most people travelling to this region for the first time, but not me, since it has traditions coming from the highly consolidated Nigerian Yoruba culture. This ancient African society settled in this area in the colonial era because of slavery and has now built its reputation across the world.

Among the main Yoruba festivals that stand out in Palmira are the Fiesta de Santa Bárbara and the Procession de Santa Barbara, dedicated to one of the town's most beloved Orisha deities. We spent the whole day there and returned later that evening. Having grown up in Nigeria and toured Cuba and other parts of the world, I've been able to relearn important values like patience and flexibility simply because they are necessary qualities to survive. I always value this reminder; it makes me a little more cheerful and less prone to road rage or commuter frustrations.

Because I live in Switzerland, it's easy to forget the comfortable things I take for granted. It's always the simple things—drinking tap water, throwing toilet paper in the toilet, sleeping without the sounds of stray animals—that seem the most luxurious to me upon coming home after a trip abroad.

When I thought of Cuba before my first visit, charming certainly was not the first word that came to mind. Elusive? Yes. Communist? Yes. I thought of both words right away. However, upon returning home, the most common word I use to describe Cuba is charming. It was indeed a charming experience for me.

E K E S U G I E | 1 5

Thomas, my brother, was the most influential person in the early stages of my life. Nature, leaving a 5-year gap between the two of us. Most siblings quarrel a lot and hardly do anything together. That was never the case for us; Thomas and I were raised differently, and we did most things together before he departed for boarding school. Throughout my young adult life, I have modelled myself to be more like him; he is not only my older brother but also my peer and my role model.

In 1983, when he was just 11 years old, his world was shaken by the deportation of over 2 million West African migrants from Nigeria, including 1 million Ghanaians. This mass deportation was because of an unjust executive order by President Shagari, the first "democratically" elected president of the second Nigerian republic. This order targeted "undocumented" immigrants, forcing them to leave the country or face arrest. As a result, the woven nylon tote bags used by most Ghanaian migrants to carry their belongings back to their country became known as the now famous "Ghana Must Go" bags.

That same year, Thomas experienced significant personal changes as well. He was in his final year of primary school at the University of Benin Staff School (UBSS) and took various common entrance exams, including those for Military School Zaria (NMS) and Air Force Military School Jos (AFMS). Unknown to him then, he would pass the exam for AFMS and attend a 2-week "interview" in Jos with boys his age from all over Nigeria. This event marked my brother's first striking experience away from home since he had moved to Nigeria at the age of four in 1975 with his Swiss mother and older sister.

In August 1983, 12-year-old Thomas began his time at AFMS, and his life as a civilian came to a close. The initial 6 months at AFMS were tough as he struggled to adapt to the new environment. The weekdays typically began with a 1-kilometre jog at four in the morning, while Saturdays were reserved for random punishments, including rolling over for up to 50 metres and performing countless push-ups, often accompanied by flogging. The boys at AFMS were brutally transformed into fearless young men, prepared to give their lives to the nation.

After 6 months of rigorous military training, which included combat training with a rifle, my brother was sworn in and pledged his oath of service to the Nigerian Air Force. At the end of 1983, Nigeria underwent a military coup that ousted the democratically re-elected government of President Shagari and installed Major General Buhari, who was later elected as a democratic president in 2015 and re-elected in 2019.

The new military regime declared a "War Against Indiscipline" (WAI), leading to the arrest, detention, and jailing of many politicians and journalists.

I remember him recounting his experiences at AFMS. I couldn't help but wonder how he felt having the same head of state at the age of twelve, who had once overthrown the government and caused unrest in his life, now acting as a godfather to the recently s-elected president, Tinubu, who he rigged elections for after completing his 8 disastrous years in office. To me, this only shows the absence of democratic growth and progress in

Nigeria, and all the more reason Nigerians should strive for 'real' change in our leadership.

Thomas was always my hero, and when I was young, around 5 or so, I would follow him everywhere; I was the pesky younger brother. My stalker attitude could be seen as a good or bad thing. I was exposed to many things I may not have known by hanging out with my brother and his friends. This was a good thing for me because it helped me mature earlier. I was able to see some of the mistakes he made and avoid them early in life. Because of him, I understood what failure was and why I must never lose my motivation when faced with it.

You see, "Failing on my dreams" is a well-known script to me. I know what it's like to fail. I've seen my elder brother Thomas, who failed many times in his life. But by seeing him, I've also learned that failure is not the opposite of success. It's a part of success. My elder brother is an inspiration to me. He dreams of becoming a successful attorney. He knows it won't be easy, but he is determined to achieve his goal.

He learns from his failures and keeps trying his best to improve. To me, this is the true spirit of a successful person.

Everyone fails once or multiple times at some point in their lives. It's what you do after you fail that matters. My brother doesn't let his failures discourage him. He uses them as an opportunity to learn and grow. He showed me that it is possible to achieve your dreams if you work hard and never give up.

I remember the moment that defined his life. It started in January 1993, when Nigeria's military Head of State, General Babangida, was restructuring the Armed Forces Ruling Council (AFRC), which he had established after the 1985 Nigerian coup d'état, where he overthrew General Buhari.

Babangida replaced the AFRC with the National Defence and Security Council (NDSC) as the supreme decision-making body of his military regime. He also appointed Shonekan as Head of the Transitional Council and Head of Government, a body designed to lead a scheduled handover to an elected democratic leader in the 1993 presidential election.

On June 12, 1993, the presidential election took place. Although the results were not officially declared by the National Electoral Commission (NEC), it was clear that Abiola and Kingibe of the Social Democratic Party (SDP) defeated Tofa and Ugoh of the National Republican Convention (NRC) by over 2.3 million votes. However, General Babangida annulled the election, citing "electoral" irregularities. This decision led to widespread protests and political unrest in the South West region, Abiola's stronghold, as many believed that Babangida had ulterior motives and did not want to cede power to Abiola.

The ongoing crisis caused by the annulled election eventually led to General Babangida's resignation in August 1993. Before his resignation, he had signed a decree establishing an Interim National Government led by Shonekan. As interim president, Shonekan initially appointed Abiola as his Vice President, but Abiola refused to recognise the interim government. The crisis persisted for months and eventually led to General Abacha seizing power on November 17, 1993.

This series of events led to a defining moment for Thomas, who could not continue his 200-level Agricultural Economics studies at the University of Benin (Uniben) because of the lingering political unrest and closure of universities. Thomas also faced personal challenges that sealed his fate, such as an incident in which a fellow student living next door in their famous off-campus residence, nicknamed the "White House," was brutally attacked by an opposing fraternity gang.

The attack left the area covered in blood, as it was brutal, though the attacked student and his visitors survived after the severe beatings they received. Shortly after the incident, my mother visited, and seeing the severity of her son's environment, she had no choice but to move him to our home in Ikpoba Hill. The event took a massive toll on Thomas, as he was in shock and couldn't stop talking about the incident for days. The family had to make a very huge decision considering the political instability in Nigeria at the time and the rise of cultism and fraternities in her universities. On September 1st, 1993, Thomas was flown back to Switzerland, where he was born in 1971 and has lived there ever since.

Looking back at these defining moments in my brother's life and seeing the present state of things in Nigeria, it's hard to say things have changed because they have not. There are still large political protests in the country's southeast region, and cultism has not changed or been reduced in the universities. In April of 2023, a four-hundred-level, final-year student of the same University of Benin was shot dead in the university's hostel (popularly known as Hall Three). This is precisely thirty years after my brother's experience.

This leaves so much to be desired in our dear country, Nigeria. I came across Buhari's speech about unity at Nigeria's 61st Independence Day.

In the speech, Buhari said, "Nigeria is for all of us. Its unity is not negotiable." That sterile cliché should have been thrown into the rhetorical refuse dump by now. "Unity" that is non-negotiable isn't unity. It's slavery. And it won't endure. Unity comes from harmony, and, as Steve Goodier reminds us, "We don't get harmony when everybody sings the same note. Only notes that are different can harmonise. The same is true with people."

Any unity that is non-negotiable is worthless and unworthy of anyone's commitment. Threatening to "take decisive actions against secessionist agitators and their sponsors," which means visiting violence on them as the regime has been doing, contradicts the earlier hope of the so-called "unity."

Secessionist agitations don't emerge out of thin air. They are activated by grievances, a profound sense of alienation, a loss of faith in the country's promises, systemic exclusion from the orbit of governance, etc. State-sanctioned violence won't stop them, and sanctimonious appeals to patriotism won't, either. What would attenuate them is deliberateness in instituting justice, fair play, inclusion, and equity.

You can't smack a child repeatedly and insist that silence in the house is non-negotiable, and that crying is an offence that will be punished with more smacking. That's both cruel and clueless.

Buhari took escapism to an undreamed-of height when he claimed that, despite glaring evidence to the contrary, "our food production capacity had increased." In which alternate universe do Buhari and his incompetent speechwriters dwell? They certainly don't live in everyday Nigeria. I understand he said all this because he was leaving office soon; maybe that is why he was trying to build an image he never had.

Buhari and his speech writers also admitted that "food prices have been going up," but attributed this "to artificial shortages created by middlemen who have been buying and hoarding these essential commodities for profiteering."

Buhari has been blaming "middlemen" for the poverty and misery his boneheaded policies have inflicted on Nigeria since his first coming as a military dictator in the eighties. He hasn't stopped. Only God knows if his successor, Bola Ahmed Tinubu, won't follow his wretched template.

For me, one of the despicable moments I've had with his undemocratic "democratic" government was the banning of Twitter. He lied and said that he suspended Twitter in Nigeria because it was "misused" as "the platform to organise, coordinate, and execute criminal activities, propagate fake news, and promote ethnic and religious sentiments".

No, I think he banned it precisely because it deleted his tweet that violated Twitter's terms and conditions, which he agreed to abide by when he signed up to use it. Twitter's action hurt his brittle ego, and he decided to carelessly suspend it, which saw Nigeria lose billions of naira in lost revenue but cost Twitter nearly zero in revenue losses.

If any proof is needed that the next few years of Buhari's successor's leadership may be worse than the past few years in which he has vandalised what remained of Nigeria, the Independence Day Speech provided it.

E N Ẹ I R R Ọ V B U G I E | 1 6

It was early in the morning of February 28, 2021, when I received a phone call from my brother, Thomas. He called to tell me about our mother's health.

How is Mother? I asked.

Not good bro, I think you should come and say your goodbyes… I have already informed Barbara.

Alright, I will join you soon, I replied as I hung up.

I couldn't believe what was going on. I sat on the couch for a few minutes, trying to summon the courage to say my goodbyes to my mother. My wife gently grabbed my shoulders from behind and stood there quietly. I was too disturbed by the moment to notice she was sobbing all along. She had found me in the saddest of times, and with the new turn of events, the next few months would be no different.

On my way to my mother's home in Bern, I was trying to nourish my thoughts with my mother's current state. The fact that she could no longer talk about her feelings stressed me a lot. I was desperate to understand her loneliness. What could be going through her mind at this point? What would she love to say to us before leaving this world? These were some questions that occupied my mind as I sat quietly on the train.

On arriving at the train station in Bern, I entered the bus, which immediately left for my mother's care home. In the following minutes, I walked my way up to the third floor, where my mother's room was. I was nervous, as if I was about to base jump the Eko Champagne Pearl Tower building in Lagos. I finally reached the front of my mother's door but couldn't find the courage to knock on it.

I stood there for a bit, observing the postcards used to decorate her room door, until I shook the nervousness off and knocked twice. As soon as I knocked, my brother Thomas opened the door, and from the look in his eyes, it was clear he hadn't been sleeping much lately. We hugged, and he walked out of the room without uttering a word. I understood all he wanted to say but couldn't find the words to express it.

As soon as he left, I was all alone with my mother, and there she was, lying unconsciously. Her bed was positioned tangentially to the window. The jalousie outside her window was dimmed, with flowers and candles beside and in front of her bed. Opposite her was a white wall. On it was a large black and white poster of our family. Even in the state she was in, she still looked beautiful. I walked to her bed, gave her a peck on her right cheek, and found a space to sit beside her. This may be the very last time I saw my mother, so I wanted to cherish every moment. Each breath she drew was a gift to me, and it then occurred to me that we humans are presented with death anytime we exhale. Why is this? We never really know if we will inhale again.

I whispered some of my thoughts in her ears occasionally as I sat close. Her hands felt cold and moist. The inner and outer circumstances of my mother's life and mine were similar, but different. Our struggles, too, have differed. Hers were the experiences of a new immigrant stranded in a strange land with no language or money to guide her. Opportunities available during the 70s to a young Swiss immigrant were limited in Nigeria, and she often felt frustrated by the limitations of her role as a Nigerian wife and mother.

My own difficulties have been more intangible. Like other men who find themselves in unexpected situations, my struggles were in different ways, similar to those of my mother.

I observed as my mother shifted around in her bed, trying to find comfort and scrunching her face. These were signs she was in pain and that time was running against me. I wanted to tell my mother something important. Something intangible and specific to me. Something she could take along on her ongoing journey to the unknown.

I held her hands softly as she breathed. She became calm, and I whispered in her ears again. "'Thank you for giving me life, mother. I promise to keep strong even while you're not here with me and maintain the great personality you've groomed for me." With these words, I stood up, clenched my fist, turned and headed towards the door. I never turned back to look. That was the last time I saw my mother 'alive.'

My mother, Klara, passed away in my brother's arms at noon on the 1st of March, 2021. The house doctor confirmed her death at twelve zero-one p.m. In order for us, the family, to carry out the necessary preparations, my mother laid in-state in her room for forty-eight hours. The same afternoon she passed away, my siblings and I sat beside her bed and watched her in silence. I think that was the longest silence I've ever experienced. I think we sat there for over ten hours.

After a long silence, Thomas got up to speak with the doctor to inquire about the next steps we had to take. He and the doctor came in to meet us where we were sitting. He handed me a bereavement leaflet and requested that I call the home bereavement team in the morning by eight a.m. They would tell me the next steps to take in obtaining the medical death certificate, which the undertakers and funeral home would require.

My mother's burial ceremony was highly emotional and beautiful. She was buried in Bern, Switzerland.

Because of the COVID-19 burial restrictions in the country, only forty people were allowed to attend the burial. However, the ceremony was also transmitted via Zoom, and over two hundred people joined in from Nigeria, the United States, the United Kingdom, China, and Switzerland.
I don't know how you can summarise or describe an entire life. There are so many intricacies. People are dynamic, and their relationships with the world are infinitely complex. My mother was a unique human being who was more than any of us could fully comprehend or describe.

When I reflect on my childhood, my mother's presence was the only consistency I had. When I remember our time together, she taught me some of life's most important lessons. And she did so in a unique but powerful way. Rarely, if ever, did she preach a specific message or compel me to act in a certain manner. Instead, my mother inspired and influenced me through her actions. While with her words, she was humble and caring, in her actions, she was bold and powerful.

When any of my friends dared question my abilities, my mother would happily correct them. When I achieved anything, she would tell the whole world. She was immensely proud. She was a true believer and protector, a Taurus mother.

With all these actions, she created the belief that ignites me daily. I think this is the best thing you can do for anyone. Believe in them. Let them surprise you with how far that belief can go.

Addressing the Stanford graduating class of 2005, the late Steve Jobs, founder and former CEO of Apple, spoke about his relationship with death: "Remembering that you are going to die," he said, "is the best way I know to avoid the trap of thinking you have something to lose. You are already naked. There is no reason not to follow your heart."

My mother, Klara, followed her heart, faced her fears, and built a legacy that remains cemented in our hearts forever.

According to Chimamanda Ngozi Adichie, who memorialised her father with her Notes on Grief, "I came to perceive grief as learning a new language."

I learned how much grief there is about a new language, its failure, and it's grasping for language. This new language, served with smug certainties, might only be perceived by people acquainted with grief.

My grief was the celebration of love between me and my mother. Those who can feel genuine grief were lucky to have loved.

For this, I am deeply grateful.

Thank you, my first true love. Klara.

Memorial Webpage of Klara Asemota.

URL
https://klara.asemota.ch

E H A I R R Ọ V B U G I E | 1 7

It was ten a.m. in Benin City. I had just gotten out of the car and was standing at the airport entrance, knowing this was the end of my visit and the start of my journey away from all the drama.

Departures were not new to me - I had done this with my parents many times before. But today was different. Only my father was alive to see me off, and honestly, the feeling was heavy in my chest.

Because of COVID-19, they didn't allow him to follow me inside for check-in. One security man with a stern-looking face approached us.

Are you going together?

No. He's my father and seeing me off.

Okay. But he will have to wait outside while you check in.

My father nodded in agreement, but I could see he was not happy at all. He touched my shoulder and said,

Take care of yourself, son. Call me when you finish.

I went inside to check in, dropped my bags, collected my boarding pass, and went back outside. When I came out, I was looking for my father everywhere. Then I saw him sitting on a metal chair, staring at the floor. The man was lost in thought.

Father!

He looked up, and his face brightened up a bit. I stood there looking at him for a few seconds before sitting with him. Both of us sat there, watching the children running up and down the hall in their childish excitement. It was a silent moment with so many words in it. With the silence, it almost felt like we were strangers, but I knew what he wanted to say to me, even though I was sure his African-parenting ego would never allow him to utter those words.

My mother's passing had left a void that exposed all the unresolved issues between my father and me. These critical moments truly tested the quality of our relationship.

There's this old saying that keeps coming back to me: "Blood makes you related; loyalty makes you family." I didn't doubt our blood connection, but the loyalty - that was completely missing.

Loyalty means trust, understanding, and feeling what the other person feels. These things were totally absent from how my father approached being a dad. This wasn't just about him - it's how many African fathers behave, always so emotionally distant.
As I raise my own sons, I'm choosing a different way. My boys - who remind me so much of my younger self - deserve a better story. They deserve to know they're seen, they're heard, and they're truly loved.

In my quiet moments, I write poems for them. I hope that one day, they'll understand my struggles and what I had to give up to be the best father I could be.

> Grandpa used to think he had it all.
> A pretty good guy, standing tall,
> But then your father came along.
> And he realised where he went wrong.
>
> Your father had some big ideas.
> Of the perfect father, without any fears,
> But life had other plans in store.
> And he had to adapt more and more.
>
> Before you all came along, my sons,
> I thought I had it all figured out.
> I thought I was a pretty decent guy.
> But then you showed up, no doubt.
>
> My hot temper and bad habits
> Were suddenly brought to light,
> I realised I had so much to learn.
> Before I could be a father right.
>
> Before you came along, my sons,
> I thought strength was all I needed.
> But then I realised, to my surprise,
> True strength comes from experience.

With you as my sons, there's no one else.
I'd rather go through life's battles with
Whether we're together or apart,
You'll always have a piece of my heart.

And now you're here, crème de scène,
A blessing like no other we've seen,
With those beautiful eyes looking up at me,
I'm filled with pride and joy, for what may be.

Grandpa learned from your father, you see,
And your father learned from you all he could be,
And now it's your turn to carry the torch.
To keep our family tree from being scorched.

So hold your heads up high, my sons.
And face life's challenges, one by one,
And never forget the lessons we've taught.
They're the roots that make us all strong as one.

My relationship with my sons is my quiet fight against my past. I want a future where fathers and sons actually enjoy each other, respect each other, and stay connected.

As a Nigerian-Swiss, I had serious problems with my father. His parenting was always like a strict manual - do this, do that, move to the next thing. Everything was just black and white. He never understood that parenting isn't about following some fixed rules.

His ideas of a man were as a provider and protector. My father was conditioned to think that his responsibilities outside our home were far more significant than those inside it. His primary concerns were my education, career prospects, and maintaining strict authority over his children.

This was how he showed love. In African father-son relationships, you don't see softness or real laughter. It's all about being serious and tough.

After my mother's memorial, I started thinking deeply. I realised I needed to see my father as more than just the man who fathered me. If I wanted to fix our broken connection, I had to understand his life before he became a father.

This was like walking through dangerous territory. One wrong step, and everything could break even more.

These problems kept pushing us apart. Many Swiss-African boys like me struggle with the same issues in their relationships with their fathers.

Considering these family dynamics, one might ask: "How do you handle this whole father-son thing—where Father meets Son, Son becomes Man, Man becomes Father, and Father turns Grandfather?"

The real problem was my father's complete refusal to understand the different world I grew up in. We might have the same blood, but our understanding came from totally different experiences. It was foolish to think we would automatically see things the same way.

Nigerian homes are complicated spaces born from our post-colonial experience. Children raised in this environment naturally pick up a modern perspective shaped by Western education, the internet, and a mixed-up cultural reality. This always creates serious conflicts with traditional African ways of thinking, leading to situations that seem impossible to resolve.

As sons of African parents living abroad, we are left to deal with this tricky situation alone. I'm Nigerian-Swiss, but my father still believes that my experiences are only shaped by our home in his ancestral land, Nigeria. The big problem with African fathers is that they ignore how our lives outside these homes completely change how we see the world.
There's always this expectation that we must rise to African thinking without them trying to understand our mixed-up perspective. We need to accept that cultures blend - it's a fool's errand to raise a wholly 'African' child in the Western nations we've made our new home.

According to South African author and academic Christopher E.W. Ouma, sons in Africa are born into an ancestral order and inherit their father's legacy like some kind of relay race. While this opinion may be similar to what is happening in many Western cultures, its application in an African context is the real issue. Ouma also suggests that the world has changed, and fresh stories are being written that challenge how African fathers used to think. And I think this applies to me.

Living in Switzerland, I've found the freedom to be different and to go against the group thinking that's so deep in many African societies. I don't have to think like my elders just because they're older.

Sure, shared beliefs can help society move forward, but having a different opinion shouldn't be seen as rebellion. We shouldn't get in trouble for speaking what we genuinely believe is right.

I'm not fully Swiss, not fully Nigerian, not fully anything. I'm caught in between, seeing more of the world, which gives me the power to question the rules we're supposed to follow. In my case, it was about challenging those old-school ideas of how a son should be, and any time I did so, the words "you don't have respect" were thrown around.

I'm not against respect, but in my home, it was a weapon my father used to shut down any argument. It was his way of avoiding responsibility and controlling everything. Over time, African parents have twisted this word, mixing it up with that Bible passage that talks about honouring your parents.
I'm not saying we shouldn't 'honour' our parents. But it's painful how people use this religious stuff to cover up their nonsense. African parents act like they can never be wrong, and that's where the problem is. The child always gets blamed, and if you try to say anything different, they call you disrespectful. We're forced to accept this crazy situation where our parents can do no wrong.

I remember sitting with my wife, telling her stories about my childhood with my father. Until that day, I had never known she understood me that much. As I concluded the story I told her, she said, "You see how all this has affected you?"

I thought about her comment deeply and realised that I had not evaluated how my father's influence had affected me. She pointed out how I get defensive quickly, overreact, and get nervous in certain situations—all because of my tough relationship with my father. I knew these things about myself but never connected them to my childhood.

Think about it, she said. We learn how to relate with people through our relationships with our parents and family. Everything - good or bad - shapes us.

She shared a Bell Hooks quote that says, "Our parents thought that patriarchal authority was always right and that children really held the same status as slaves whose primary task was to obey".

This quote describes how my siblings and I saw our father. There was no space for discussions, and we were expected to obey without question.

Men like your father don't understand, she continued, that by being so tough, they miss the chance to have proper conversations with their children.

She painted a picture of an environment where children could voice their thoughts without fear of judgment and where fathers could admit their mistakes. This was not a complete dismantling of the father-son hierarchy, which is very important in every parental relationship, but creating grounds where children can connect with their fathers and learn from their mistakes as they become adults, just like I learned from my brother, Thomas.

She leaned back on the couch we were sitting on and said,

But there is another angle to all of these, too.

She was right. My father was born in Nigeria 30 years before we got freedom from the British. You can only imagine how toxic those periods were - everyone fighting for their freedom, and there's also the Biafra War to consider. All these affected how my father was raised and the kind of love he received from his own father.

I do not know my grandfather that much, but I can guess that he couldn't waste time thinking about how to respect his son's emotions while in the midst of a civil war. His job was just to keep the family alive, make sure they got an education, and have food to eat. This hard way of being a father, formed during tough times, was passed down to my father—and he never changed it.

In the mid-1960s, he moved to Germany and Switzerland. Those days, racism wasn't hidden - it was everywhere. Working minor jobs and struggling to survive - all this destroyed his confidence. Our home became his only place of control.

Because of his tough life, he had no time to create a new parenting style and had to rely on his father's methods, which were built based on control and survival. He didn't have the chance to think about emotions like we do now. For him, keeping the family stable was the only thing that mattered.

As I approach 50, I understand how tough life can be for a father. I see now the battle's my father might have fought alone, the wounds he probably never healed. The painful truth is that I don't really know my father. Our lack of real conversations has created a massive wall of misunderstanding between us. Though our relationship might be unstable, I've come to accept him for who he is and love him despite his imperfections.

At least my generation is changing the narratives about parenting. We understand the emotional damage our parents caused even though they never meant to, and we're employing a different strategy for our own children. All this talk about mental health and what it means to be a man is changing everything. We're not going to parent like our fathers did.

We've copied our fathers in ways we know and don't know. It's time to stop these old habits. Being emotional is not a weakness. Men can't keep hiding behind this tough-guy nonsense. Society will keep pushing this old-school man thing, but we shouldn't accept it.

Being a father is more than just making babies or being around. It's about building a good human, helping them feel strong inside, and teaching them genuine character. That's what fatherhood should be.

Suddenly, the airport speakers came alive. "Flight 1057 now boarding," they announced. I was pulled back to reality from my deep thoughts.

My father and I stood up. Our movements were stiff, full of things we never said. We hugged quickly—no promises, no sorry, just a quick recognition of how far apart we really were.

My heart was beating hard as I walked to the airport entrance. Each step felt heavy. I looked back one last time, wanting to remember something about my father. But he was gone. He had disappeared amid hundreds of people walking around, just like any hope we had of getting close.

I left Benin City on a flight bound for Switzerland, my mind heavy with uncertainty. I had no idea when I would see my father again. I knew he would not be visiting us in Switzerland. The trip to Nigeria, which I had hoped would mark a new chapter in our relationship, had only widened the gap between us.

A realisation dawned on me - boys do not yearn for their fathers' masculinity; they yearn for their fathers' hearts. But my father never gave me that. And it hurt badly.

As the plane took off, I was leaving more than just my father. I was leaving behind the last bit of hope I had for the father-son relationship I always wanted.

E V A I R R O̞ V B U G I E | 1 8

It's nine forty-five a.m., and I'm back in Switzerland. Was my journey what I expected it to be? Perhaps. I was not expecting much from the whole bonding thing; in fact, I had already guessed how it would end.

It's almost like I regret returning to Nigeria because nothing changed. Not my relationship with my father, and certainly not my experiences as a multicultural person in a black-populated country like Nigeria.

People like me are very easy to target in a place like Nigeria; however, what picture does a person of my skin tone paint? Plenty!

I am someone who grew up in a culture where people of fair complexion were a small minority. I mean, Nigeria is beautiful and black, just the way I love it. But the fact is, white or fair people were hard to find in the 1970s in places like Benin City. I always felt ambiguous about the attention directed to me, my siblings, my mother, and also people from the Fulani tribe in the north of Nigeria (who somehow had the same skin tone as me). I have always felt that urge to know the experiences of not only multicultural people with fair complexions but also light-skinned people (like the Fulanis).

Having a multicultural identity in Nigeria or Switzerland sometimes gave me the sense of 'feeling very other' and 'un-placeable in people's minds,' which brought many difficulties when I was growing up. This feeling and experience manifested itself in my relationships with my father, uncles, aunts, class teachers, a couple of friends, and the world.

In Nigeria, these difficulties manifested differently, or rather oppositely, than in Switzerland, in terms of their effect on me. Special treatment was one of the many difficulties or subtle discrimination I experienced while strolling through the streets of Benin City. I never had a feeling I was being rejected in these awkward moments. I just felt I was treated as another tribe. I also noticed this pattern with other ethnic groups in Nigeria.

Although the feeling of 'otherness' is universal and exists in all communities, with multicultural people like me, it is often emphasised by the environment, which makes it seem even more problematic.

On the contrary, my experiences in Switzerland and other European countries felt rejective. I would probably consider a large percentage of the special treatment experiences as 'humiliating.' I still come in contact with people today (in Europe and America) who believe I have no academic path or feel I am less versed or experienced in what I do. Others expressed their thoughts and imaginations on what my classroom in Nigeria looked like. They imagined me sitting on a tree branch and holding my book with one hand.

Thanks to my mother, I was born in Benin City, Nigeria, and I also have her to thank for the beautiful childhood I experienced. She was very adventurous. She fell in love with my father in London, a very exotic city. In the 1960s, falling in love with a black man was in itself an unthinkable project for some white people. But little did they know they would raise their family in Nigeria. Well, of course, after giving birth to my siblings overseas.

I can still remember when the decision for me to move to Switzerland came; it was like a movie, or should I say, "It dropped like a stone on a glass table." I initially didn't buy the idea, but my parents (especially my father) were insistent. And I don't blame them.

Because of the poor academic situation in West Africa, Nigeria's political backwardness, and the particular context I found myself in back then, my father decided it would be best for me to pursue my studies in Switzerland. This decision was non-negotiable.

As in any Nigerian household back then, the man of the house (in this case, my father) always had the final say. So, his decision was final for me. I had no room to air my feelings or even discuss the details of my relocation. In that period, I became versed in the scenarios of letting go and starting all over again. I left many good friends behind. Some of them I lost; others felt abandoned by me.

Most of my friends who didn't have the same options as me remained in Nigeria and eventually graduated with a degree (and we still communicate frequently to this day). That said, in retrospect, the academic situation was not as bad as my father thought it was.

The choice by my father to move me out of Nigeria was one of many factors that put a huge bridge into our relationship. My parents lost their last son in exchange for hope and a better life in Switzerland. And you cannot blame them for that. A better life is all a parent can wish for their child. But for an eighteen-year-old back then, it was hard. 29 years later, I still feel like Nigeria deprived me of a better relationship with my parents.

Even though I travelled regularly to Switzerland as a child, I still felt like a complete foreigner when I arrived in Zurich at 18. This cancerous feeling I had of being a foreigner was painful to me. After all, Switzerland was my home—the home of my mother. I had to reconstruct this completely abandoned and nearly empty Swiss part of me. Life situations and external facial parameters I possessed didn't help either. One part of me was Nigerian, the other Swiss. Swiss people always saw the Nigerian in me, as I didn't look like a typical Swiss. The answer to what a typical Swiss or Nigerian should look like is left to you to evaluate.

It is 2024, and I am still reconstructing my Swiss side. Being multicultural instilled a kind of disorder in me. I would compare it with schizophrenia. One part of me resonates with the country of Nigeria, and the other is with Switzerland. I automatically feel at home on the Nigerian side of me, not only because I was born there, but also because it is the side that suffers.

Suffer, in the sense that Europeans colonised Nigeria. Hence, the white side of me colonised the black side of me. Crazy, you would imagine, but it is just a reality I have to live with.

My multicolour experience shifted my perspective and personal philosophy about life to a broader position. Broadened by self-questioning and investigation, the Ubuntu philosophy embodied and deepened the connection to the origins of the human experience. What I learned from Ubutu is that we are not separate. Placing our values on compassion, community, generosity, and mutual support will help us unite and move forward as persons, countries, or people of the world. This pro-social behaviour is why humans have become the dominant species. It is the essence of what makes us humans.

To contribute towards a post-racial future, I can assert that people of colour need to "counter the negativity". Our society is changing fast, so we should consider how our identities can help bring that narrative forward. Multicultural people are on the cutting edge of today's culture, which has moved on from segregation to acceptance.

Belgium, the United Kingdom, France, Germany, Italy, Japan, the Netherlands, Portugal, and Spain colonised African countries, with Spain having at least 32 colonies and the United Kingdom about 90. The slave trade lasted for at least 400 years, if not more. Not to mention other victims like the Inca Empire, the Clovis of America, or Aboriginal people from Australia.

None of these colonist countries have been called to account for their crimes against humanity. Many German generals have been indicted and charged with crimes they started and executed against the Jewish people, which I think was the right call. These warmongering generals truly deserved the punishment for their evil and uncultured quest for power and dominance.

But I can't recall any of the above-colonised countries being indicted by an International Military Tribunal or any other tribunal for their crimes against Africa. Why is this? I still cannot find the answer!

Africans are the only race of people who are told to forget their history. Forget the slave trade. Told to forget the past and move on.

It is important to know that colonisation was never a matter of coincidence or chance. It was rather a premeditated move of the colonial powers, motivated by the aim of exploiting the economic and political benefits of another country.

White supremacy is the pre-existing condition that has made the slave trade deadlier for people of colour and simultaneously held back the economic recovery of countries that were victims of the slave trade.

It is all confusing for me. Colonists arrived on the African continent, ransacked it, incited confusion, destroyed their social, economic, and political systems, instilled more confusion, and then left. All this is to enable colonists to maintain power over Africa.

I have no problem with whites, nor do I have any problems with other tribes or races. My mother was white, but she never felt or showed that she was inherently superior to the Nigerians during her 40-year stay in Nigeria. Yet, I wonder why it was different with the colonisers. Why did they have to push the notion that their skin was better than others and their intellect was superior?

Thoughts and questions like these do not have answers, because no one is there to answer them. However, these thoughts have led me to put together a piece of poetry that goes:

> I see the burdens my homeland has weathered.
> Once vibrant cultures had faded and drained,
> As Western norms planted their standard unattained.
>
> Once lands of gods like Zeus, Ọlọrun, and more
> Now crosses and crescents reign; other faiths are ignored.
> Even skin is now ranked by tones; lighter is prized, it seems.
> Beauty is defined by Western norms; our braids are called unclean.
> Fashion answers the Paris runways; Hollywood sets the scene.
>
> Academia crowns Harvard; status is defined by Sheen.
> Music seeks the Grammys' glory, and films yearn for Oscar's nod.
> Art is only seen as artful if the West applauds.
>
> Adichie shines but by measures set by the colonial yardstick.
> Our democracy is modelled on the colonisers' quick trick.
> There's little room for our rhythms, and the structures are all pre-set.

Centuries later, the white way remains hard-begotten.

Two heritages spin within; glory and theft entwine.
The empire celebrates gains off my ancestors' spine.
Can a new path yet emerge in peace, not dominance?
Respecting all wisdoms, not just the West's standard?

While poetry may be a beautiful way to express hidden thoughts and address displeasing topics, it can only change a little if the people it addresses do not take its words to heart and act on them.
I firmly believe Nigeria is not a failed state, but a sabotaged nation. To fail, we would have to try, and change is always imminent. The suffering in Nigeria is too much, so we must take action to change things.

A Benin proverb goes, "Erokhi ma mien ebe, ele" —if the chameleon does not see danger, it does not run. That said, all the chameleons have left Nigeria, and all the talents have run away. And I can't blame them. Nigeria is not a stable environment to grow because we have consistently witnessed upheavals in politics and social life.

But who is going to fix things if we all leave? My best guess is no one—absolutely no one! So, the only option left is to figure things out so that our kids can have a place to call home and be proud of when they trace back to their roots.

So, what can we do? We can start by becoming more Nigerian-oriented and removing our reliance on white-centric conditions and influences. We need to wake up in the morning without wanting to be like Warren Buffett or Mark Zuckerberg, but instead, we dream of becoming the next Oba Ovonramwen Nogbaisi.

After 60 years of mining oil in Nigeria, why don't we have any domestic processing and refinery infrastructure to purify our oil and sell our own petrol from our soil? The fossil fuel giant Shell has devastated and polluted many water sources in many villages in Nigeria, and you can't question their destructive behaviour because they are not an African-centred company; they are only here for profits. So, we need more Nigerians to step up and become their competition.

Congo roughly accounts for 70% of global cobalt production, and Nigeria also produces cobalt. Why can't our young businessmen and women leverage our cobalt production to start the next EV vehicle brand that will rival Tesla? When will Nigerians understand that the story of Mary Slessor was just a subjugation act by the British? How can she stop the killing of twins when young children identified as witches are being put on fire in England?

Before we, as a people, can change our nation, we must first reprogram our minds and not act like zombies. My favourite outspoken artist and musician, Fela Aníkúlápó Kuti, once released a song titled "Zombie" back in 1976, criticising the oppressive military regime in Nigeria. In the song, Fela Kuti compares the Nigerian military personnel to zombies who follow orders mindlessly.

As citizens, we need to wake up to our true selves and leverage the power of our creative minds. Only then can we change the narrative and gain the respect we deserve. So I say:

> Wake Up, Nigerians, Wake Up!
> Shake off the slumber of mindless consumption,
> Break free from the trance of cultural zombies.
> Our beauty lies not in mere aesthetics,
> But in the power to forge our own path.
>
> Too long have we been followers, consumers,
> Chasing after foreign trends and standards.
> It's time to mind our own business,
> To create, to build, to set our own bar.
>
> Let us embrace our rich heritage,
> Nurturing homegrown businesses with pride.
> Instead of designer bags, let's carry
> The weight of our nation's prosperity.
>
> No more living for fleeting moments,
> But planning for generations to come.
> Our cobalt riches hold no value
> Until we forge our own devices, our own might.
>
> Wake Up, Nigerians, Wake Up!
> Become the merchants, the makers, the pioneers.
> Let our power radiate from within,
> Crafting a legacy that forever inspires.

As Damini Ebunoluwa said, a mental revolution is needed to change our beloved country. Brainwashed people who still believe in privileges, corruption, and fairytale stories of how powerful the white man is cannot create or maintain progress.

We need to eradicate corruption and corrupt leaders. We also have to understand that privilege goes hand in hand with corruption. We need to drop the privileged attitude, shed tribalism and bigotry, and work towards ensuring that all achievements are merit-based. Treat everyone with respect and kindness (irrespective of their skin colour or economic level). We don't need government intervention for simple stuff like this.

Corruption can be beaten if we work together. To stamp out the abuse of power and bribery and shed light on secret deals, citizens must come together to tell their governments they have had enough (Jose Ugaz, 2015). This is how we must start the revolution to make Nigeria the giant it is.

G l o s s a r y

Online Glossary of Pidgin English words used in this book shared as a Notion Webpage. Notion is a productivity note-taking web application.

URL
https://screeching-sleep-07e.notion.site/14c8a07f7841802a9705e6673521ec54?v=14c8a07f784181199fce000c643595dc

A B O U T   T H E   A U T H O R

Stefan Asemota was born in 1976 at the University of Benin Teaching Hospital (UBTH) in Benin City, Nigeria. He completed his early education at the University of Benin Staff School and his West African Examination Council (WAEC) exams at the University Demonstration Secondary School in Benin City.
He then moved to Switzerland to further his education, and today, he is an internationally certified Interior Carpenter, Software Engineer, and Scrum Master. Beyond his professional achievements, he is a dedicated family man, happily married with children.

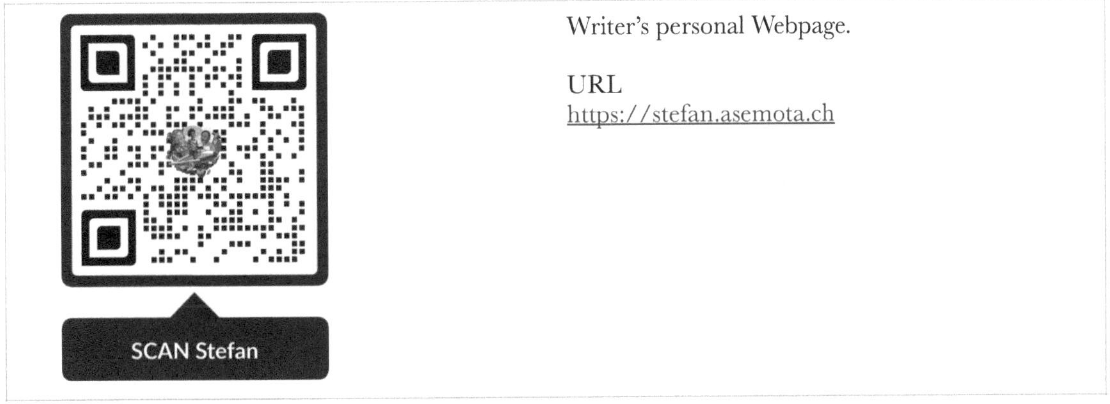

Writer's personal Webpage.

URL
https://stefan.asemota.ch

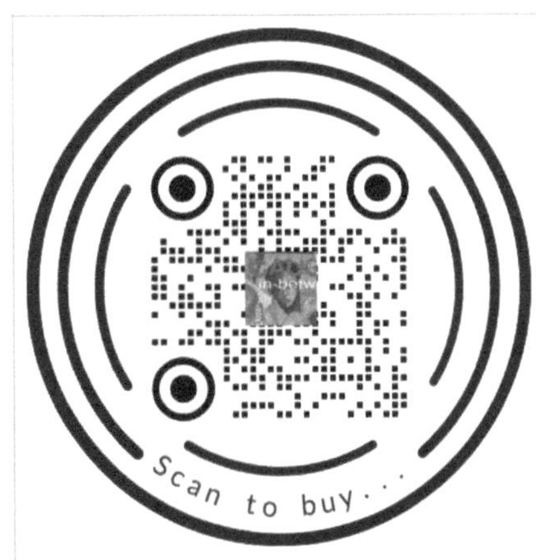

Caught In-Between on Amazon.

URL
https://www.amazon.com/o/ASIN/ 373924805X/lovebook-detail-21? ref=d6k_applink_bb_dls&dplnkId=a76a8fbc-3ce3 -4913-a25d-526694982f87

Caught In-Between

Stefan Asemota
ISBN-13: 978-3739248059

Still hoping to be long listed for the Caine Prize for African Writing

'Stefan coaxes us into his life journeys; riddled with uncertainties, encountered in his quest for balance and meaning! The beauty of this script would be all the bits that resonate with you, while you get to enjoy the scintillating narrative and descriptive style employed to teleport you into his Nigerian and life experience, which was laughter, joy, sad and mad, all in one Long Cocktail, guaranteed to intoxicate.'
London, United Kingdom

'In a brutally honest narrative, the author takes us on a mentally intriguing cultural journey with a front-view of his life as a man who lost his mother, trying to understand his father while redefining how the world thinks and how his home country, Nigeria, can be better. There are certainly books you can skip on, but not this one.'
Lagos, Nigeria

'Great book about Nigeria from a perspective from a Nigerian-Swiss'
Lisboa, Portugal

B O O K   M E R C H

During the course of writing this book, I was inspired to bring some of the characters to life.

As an Apparel designer for almost half a decade, I believe it's a responsibility to create designs that are not only aesthetically pleasing but also environmentally conscious. I am excited to contribute to our World, where fashion can be both stylish and sustainable.

This inspiration motivated me to collaborate with a fantastic artist from Lagos, Nigeria.

Feel free to check out the items for yourself!

Writer's Merchandise e-Commerce Shop.

URL
https://asemota.etsy.com